MW01622717

Reach Beyond the Break

The Avery Johnson Story

As Told to Jimmie Hand

A & D Publishing

Printed in The United States of America

04 03 02 01 00 1 2 3 4 5

Library of Congress Catalog Number XXXXXX

ISBN: 0-9722745-0-2

Cover Design Jonathan Gullery

Cover Photos and photos on pages 6,26,38,46,84,93 courtesy of NBA Photos

A&D Publishing
The Woodlands, Texas

I want to dedicate this book to my parents, Jim and Inez Johnson who are in Heaven saying, "We are proud of you son!"

And to Cassandra, my wife who has stood by my side unconditionally. Thank You!

Avery Johnson

Table of Contents

Christmas 1999 AJ takes a shot during a game with the Los Angeles Lakers at Staples Center in LA Donald Miralle/All Sport

Reach Beyond the Break

Chapter One

Reaching

Psalm 73:23
"Yet I am always with you;
You hold me by my right hand."

The temperature was near ninety degrees and the humidity was even higher on a hot Sunday morning in Houston, Texas, and the people of Brentwood Baptist church were gathering for the morning worship service.

Some were dressed in their finest, the men in summer suits and the ladies wearing sleeveless summer dresses. Others had on blue jeans and t-shirts. About half of the women wore stylish hats as was the custom in the Southwest.

The glass-enclosed marquee stood on a little grassy knoll in front of the large brick church displaying a cross on top of a steeple. The sign read:

Brentwood Baptist Church
Sunday School at 8:30
Morning Worship at 9:45
Guest Speaker—Avery Johnson

The people greeted each other and found their way to their favorite places in the pews where they greeted more friends with handshakes and hugs . . . lots of hugs.

The worship service lasted about ninety minutes, and the congregation surely felt the presence of the Holy Spirit. Pastor Joe Ratliff came to the pulpit and introduced the guest speaker.

"Folks, we are privileged to have as our speaker this morning a young man that has dedicated his life to the work of the Lord. Many of you know him as an NBA basketball player, which he has been for almost eight years, but today you will hear and see another side of Avery Johnson."

With that the congregation stood and gave Avery a standing ovation. "Thank you. You are too kind," he said with that million - dollar smile "but lets give the glory to Jesus who makes it all happen."

As the people settled into their seats, Avery asked them to join him in prayer. It was a short humble prayer of thanks to God for who He is and to ask His blessing on the service.

"Many of you know me as a basketball player, but when you see that I have to look up to most of you, you're not sure that the NBA I play in is the same one you see on TV."

That brought laughter from the congregation. Avery stood in silence with his head bowed for several seconds then he said, "Thank you Lord. Praise Your name!"

There were a number of "Amen's" and "Yes, yes" from the people.

"This morning, I hope and pray that what I will tell you will encourage those that need encouragement and give peace to those of you that are searching for it. It is my desire that you come to a point where your . . . faith is so strong that you will know—you'll just **know** that God is in control."

Again the amen's and yes's from the people.

"Let me tell you about a song that I heard several years ago that inspired me." Now I'm not going to sing it but the words go something like this.

The congregation all laughed.

There was an old man who was taking his grandson out fishing in a small boat on a beautiful little lake. The little boy was so excited—so excited. He was with his grandfather and they were having fun. Neither of them could swim, but they went out on this little boat anyway.

As the little boy tried hard to land a fish he leaned over the side of the boat too far and fell in the water. Once he fell in he knew he was in trouble because he couldn't swim. The grandfather couldn't swim either. But the grandfather found a small rope lying in the back of the boat. Holding on to one end of the rope, he threw the other end to the boy. And the little boy grabbed the rope and was relieved as his grandpa began pulling him into the boat.

Then all of a sudden the rope started breaking just a few inches from where the boy held on for dear life, and the grandfather said some of the most profound words that I have ever heard in my life. He said, **"Reach beyond the break**." The boy did, and the boy was saved.

"That's what I want to talk to you all about this morning. *Reach beyond the break,* at home, on your job, in your past, at school, with your wild children at home . . . Yes, outwardly you are sharp but internally, secretly, behind closed doors you need to *reach beyond the break.*

Maybe it' s your health, not necessarily because you smoke or you need to give up some sin that's breaking you down.

I can promise you this—if you take one step God will take two! You can't just stand there with a broken rope in your hand! You do your best and God will do the rest. It's a two way street. It's not all God and it's not all you. It's what we call a covenant relationship.

Many times in my young life I've had to *reach beyond the break.* Times when I didn't want to! Times when it didn't feel safe to let go of the rope! It just didn't!

The congregation was full of sighs and Praises to the Lord

as he finished the story.

"That song reminds me of my own life. It seems that from the time I was born on March 25th 1965 in New Orleans, Louisiana in the Lafitte Projects that I have always been facing a fraying rope and have had to ask God to give me the strength to *reach beyond the break.*

My young life was not what one would call easy. The areas in New Orleans are divided up into Wards and mine was the Sixth Ward. Growing up in the 6th ward in the projects would cause anyone to wonder how a young man could survive such a beginning. The projects were huge, covering about eight square blocks. There were shootings and drugs being used and dealt almost everywhere. You'd hear a shooting at night and the next morning you'd get up and find out so and so had been shot.

The main problem was outsiders. They would come in and cause all kinds of trouble. But the people in our neighborhood respected one another. I wasn't afraid living in the projects because we were all pretty much like family. Even though some of the people in my projects were doing illegal things they didn't bother us. They were always respectful to my mom and dad. They were respectful of our environment. I don't think our projects were any nicer than those of New York or Chicago or any other big city. And I don't think they were any rougher either. I always had an optimistic attitude. The glass is always half full in my eyes.

In the projects there were a lot of fatherless children for one reason or another and this contributed to many of the problems. Kids that didn't have fathers were more likely to be the ones getting into trouble. They didn't perform as well in school as the other kids. There was a lot of loneliness, a lot of depression and because of that loneliness and depression there were drugs.

Another problem was that the kids without fathers were having children out of wedlock early in life. Some of the girls having babies were just children themselves. Statistics show that 50 to 60 percent of men in jail didn't know their fathers and that's a major problem. There were just no good role models in their lives. I was scared to death to let my daddy down so I never got into any of that just because of his influence

But my mother and father filled my life with a deep love that helped me overcome many challenges that would have gotten to me without their love and support. One of the biggest obstacles that I always seemed to face was my height. I was just so much shorter than the other guys that it was always an uphill battle. My dad always encouraged me. He'd say, "You know it's not how big you are physically, it's how big your heart is." And my mom would tell me things like, "You may not be big but you sure are fast. You're still my son, and I believe in you."

I also had to get help from my dad regarding girls. At one time I was dating a girl in high school, but then in my senior year of college I met Cassandra—my future wife. I had a big, big decision to make, and my dad helped me make it. The problem was that I loved both of them. My dad showed me how to make the right choice.

And when it came time for me to get a job my dad helped me decide on what job to take. I thought I wanted to be a waiter and make lots of money—you know with tips and all. But my dad talked me into taking a job with Crescent Plywood for less money. It turned out well because Norman Chenevert, the owner of Crescent Plywood, became a true mentor to me.

My dad made me take that job, and it was a lot harder than being a waiter. I had to handle concrete, and I loaded sheet rock and plywood onto trucks all summer and it was 99 degrees in the warehouse!

Of course I was poor in material things, and there were a lot of obstacles, but it was the same with all of my other friends and their families. What I remember about that time was mostly that there just weren't a lot of extras. I just didn't have a lot of extra stuff. The clothes I started the school year with were the ones I ended it with. The tennis shoes I started the year with I finished the year with. I couldn't just think about myself. I always had to think about the family.

When I went to the refrigerator to get a drink of orange juice, I had to think about four, five, or six people coming after me, so I couldn't drink it all up. It was always a limited supply that never quite met the demand.

Sometimes I had to use a little hot water when I took a bath so others following me had hot water. With one bathroom, it seemed that if I was taking a bath someone needed to use the toilet, and they couldn't wait so there I was taking a bath and having to endure the odors.

We always celebrated birthdays, Christmas, Easter and the likes, but it wasn't with any extravagant parties. Most of the presents were hand made. Maybe they were made at school by classmates or teachers or maybe at home. We made many more things than we bought. Today we're into buying things, but back then we made things. My mother would bake our birthday cakes, but now we go to the store and buy a fancy already-made cake. Now it's "I'll buy you a gift," but back then it was "I'll make you a gift." It's been a big change.

Christmas was always a big thing for us kids. My dad worked hard and saved up. But it was always hard. My parents would go into debt trying to buy all those presents, so I remember that January was always our worst month. My dad had saved and then spent the money on presents. He'd run up the credit card, and then came January and he had to pay it back. And besides, January was always a slow month in my dads carpenter work with the bad weather and all.

I remember we would go to a place called the Auditorium to try to get one present. They would give out one present per kid. They'd be giving away real toys and we'd get in line at five in the morning to get one present.

I was as excited then about Christmas as my kids are today just because it was Christmas. There was always that possibility of getting one toy, whereas my kids today are excited because they know they're going to get ten.

Chapter Two

Family Love

Psalm 68:6
"God sets the lonely in families,
He leads forth the prisoners with singing:
but the rebellious live in a sun-scorched land."

I was rich in the love of my father, Jim Johnson, and my mother Inez Johnson. My mother was the nicest person on the face of the earth. My mother didn't have a mean part on her body. She never used a foul word in her life. And was she a great cook! I mean the woman could cook! She cooked all those great Cajun dishes like Gumbo, Jambalaya, Shrimp Creole and my favorite, cabbage and rice.

"She was a mother! She was a wife, she was a friend and, oh she was a servant. She served my dad and her family. What a gracious servant."

My mother was forty-years old when I was born and she only worked outside of the home for a short while when I was very young, but she was always there at home when my little sister Andrea and I were growing up.

Andrea is four years younger than me, and we were the only children at home most of the time while we were growing up. We were very close in those early years. She would always go to the park where I was playing ball and I looked out for her pretty well. She was proud of me as her big brother I' m sure. We had some interesting times growing up. I remember a time when she wanted me to teach her to drive. My dad was not too sure about letting his baby learn to drive. Well to make a long story short, Andrea wanted to get behind the wheel and drive forward, but I thought it was important that she learn how to change a tire and back up. After some crying and close calls we both decided this was not the right time for her to learn to drive. We' re still close today. We talk on the phone regularly. We do Bible studies together and we pray together. We just help each other spiritually.

My hard working father provided for our family as a carpenter. He was tall—six foot three—a slender-built man who I called, "A father of fathers." He was a country boy from a town called Saint Francisville. It was a pretty small town of about five thousand people. I had visited there several times when I was young.

When we'd go down there my grandmother Kitty Johnson would make me go and feed the pigs. I'd be back there in the slop and mud feeding the pigs a kind of sloppy feed. They' d be running over me, trying to knock me down to get to the feed.

Another thing that wasn't to my liking was that my grandmother had an outhouse. There was no indoor plumbing and that outhouse . . . man it was always smelly and had lots of flies. It was disgusting!

But one really good thing I remember was that my grandmother would get up early in the morning and bake delicious biscuits. I can smell them now! She lived right off of a main highway, and you could hear the cars and trucks going by all night.

One thing I'll never forget was one time when we were visiting there and my cousin Curtis, who was a prison guard, decide to make an impression on me. He said, "Avery, lets go for a ride." So we took off and rode and rode.

We went to another little town called Angola, about twenty miles from St. Francisville. It was a dark scary road—no street lights and I'd ask, "Curtis, where are we going?" It was about a thirty-minute ride that seemed like an hour. The next thing you know we were pulling up to a massive looking building. There were lights and barbed wire. There were some lights on the sign that said Angola State Penitentiary. Along with Pelican Bay in California this was one of the worst prisons in the world. I was about eleven or twelve years old.

"This is where I work Avery." He took me in there and took me on a tour. The inmates were screaming at me. They'd say things like. "Boy, come on in here and I'll beat you up" an all kind of vulgar stuff like that. He showed me from the outside where they did the executions. My heart dropped! Then he grabbed me and said, "You know if you ever do anything bad in your life, you could end up in a place like this. You're going to have some decisions you're going to have to make in life, and if you make the wrong decisions you could end up here. You better make sure you make good decisions in your life, Avery, because I sure don't want you to end up here. This is pure hell." That scared the heck out of me I'll tell you. Curtis took me there not just to scare me but because he loved me.

Going to St. Francisville was a great family time, and Andrea, my sister, was almost always with us.

My dad didn't have much formal education but he had God-given wisdom that he shared with his family. Mom and Dad always made sure there was food on the table . . . maybe sometimes on the lean side, but it would fill your stomach. We didn't miss any meals. There were a few nights when it got a little rough, but we made it.

"My dad, my dad! My dad was an incredible man. He wasn't a perfect man but he was an incredible man!" He had been married before and divorced his first wife and left six kids behind. He told me it was one of the hardest things he ever had to do to leave his kids behind.

Chapter Three

A New Found Love

Psalm 16:11
"You have made known to me the path of life
You will fill me with joy in your presence, with
eternal pleasures at your right hand."

When I was a youngster I can still remember on Saturday morning I would be waiting for the sunlight to come up. I was waiting for the sunlight to come up so I could go put on my basketball shoes, get my basketball, and go outside and just work on my game. In the projects we had like a little blacktop court right behind my house.

I liked to get out there before anybody else. I was always out there an hour or two before any of my friends got there. I felt as though my hard work got me ahead of them. I was about ten or eleven, and when I played against my friends I could see the results of putting in the necessary time to get better. I played from sun up to sun down. Every weekend it was the same thing.

I was always small for my age, and it wasn't until I got to college that I had a bit of a growing spurt. Phyllis Wheatly elementary school was where my education started in New Orleans and I continued my schooling in New Orleans until I graduated from St. Augustine High School. The teacher that made the most impression in my early years was in the sixth grade and his name was Mr. Grandprix and he was awesome. I was a good student that didn't get into much trouble. I didn't want to have to deal with my father for getting into trouble, so I tried to do the right things. The worst thing that happened to me was getting suspended for fighting when I was in the third grade.

I first started playing basketball when I was six years old, and I took to basketball like a duck takes to water. I was also a good baseball player, and I played centerfield and pitched. I was left-handed and had the best curve ball in New Orleans.

I'll tell a funny story on "Hoss' (Joe Armant). When I was about 13-14 years old I was playing baseball on a team that was playing another team managed by Joe Armant. It was a close game—0-0 in the bottom of the last inning. I don't remember how I got to third base—maybe a double and a steal of third. Anyway here I was on third base. Joe' s third baseman went out to the pitcher and they were going to try the hidden ball trick on me, but I saw it coming all the way. I said to Hoss. "Hoss, that's the oldest trick in the book. You ain't going to fool me." Hoss said, "Well Avery we tried to fool you." He told the third baseman to give the ball back to the pitcher. The third baseman threw the ball to the pitcher but he wasn't looking and the ball got away and I ran home with the winning run. Hoss just smiled at me.

I wouldn't be totally honest if I didn't tell you about my football career. I told my dad I wanted to play football, and he always encouraged me to try new things, so he took me out and bought the equipment I would need. That first day . . . that first big hit . . . I knew if I couldn't be the kicker my football career was over. Right then and there I knew I was a basketball player.

At the Lemon Playground a guy named "Lujack" first introduced me to the game that would be a major part of my life. He had been a New Orleans high school sports star and was an outstanding athlete. At that time he ran the park. He was there to give us balls and bats and to open the swimming pool so we could swim in the warm months. He also got me started on the fundamentals of the game of basketball.

He balanced the fundamentals and running wind sprints and laps with the fun of the game. It was from him that I first learned to dribble the ball with both hands. This was not something that every six-year-old could do and that has carried me through.

Nevertheless, being a recreation leader in the Lafitte Housing Projects meant he had to do more than just hand out equipment and teach skills. He also had to be concerned for the safety of my friends and me. I can remember many times when a baseball bat accompanied Lujack to the outdoor courts. A few times he was even reported to have brought a gun to guarantee us kids safety.

It was the atmosphere that was bad, because you were always hearing gun shots or police sirens, and it wasn't uncommon to see dice games, and drug dealers around the basketball courts. It was a rough place, but it was what we had, and we made do. We had both black and white policemen. We felt it was a sure thing that you'd get a better shake from the black policemen.

The coaching I received from Lujack and the talent that God had given me soon gave me the reputation as the best player for my age on the Lemon playground.

Lujack can still be found helping kids on the playgrounds developing their skills in basketball, football, and baseball, and I'll always be thankful to him for all he did for me.

It was after Lujack had planted the seed that Joe "Hoss" Armant came along, and he was so impressed with what I could do with a basketball that he wanted me to play on his team in the NORD. (New Orleans Recreational Department). This would also be my first time ever to play in an indoor facility. The Treme Recreation Center was the first indoor sports and community center to be open in my neighborhood. The basketball leagues there were highly- competitive . . . something new to me.

Joe "Hoss' Armant was an awesome man an—awesome man! He was another great male example for me. He' s still close to me, and one whose opinion that I take to heart. He now lives in Mesquite, Texas and when I play in Dallas he always comes to my games. Now that I'm playing with the Dallas Mavericks I'm sure I'll see more of him.

He introduced me to organized basketball when I was ten years old. He saw me playing on the playgrounds and told me about Biddy Basketball. It sounded like something that I would like to try so I brought Joe home to meet my dad. He told my dad that I was really a good player, and he wanted me to play on his Biddy Basketball team. He told my dad he could teach me some fundamentals that would help me later on. My dad gave his okay, so that started me playing organized basketball. We won the downtown District Championship that year and we won the National Biddy Basketball championship too.

I played on AAU and summer teams for coach Calvin Ramie and Anthony "Tiggy" Roman. I can't think of two people who love children in New Orleans more than them. I also spent time as a ball boy at Xavier University thanks to Coach Dale Valdery. Coach Val gave me the opportunity of a lifetime. I loved catching the bus after school and going to XU. I learned a lot from two awesome small college point guards during the late 70's and early 80's named Mike Brite and Bo Dukes.

During that time basketball came pretty easy for me, and it was a lot of fun, and Joe was a great coach. Later on when I was up at Cameron University in Oklahoma I came down to Mesquite and Joe took me to a Mavericks game. It was my first time to see in person a real live NBA game, the Boston Celtics versus the Dallas Mavericks. (other than when I was a kid and we used to sneak into the New Orleans Jazz games.) We sat up in the high altitude seats but I loved it. I told Joe that night that I thought I had the game to play in the NBA.

Joe didn't want to hurt my feelings but he did point out

that it was a long way from these nosebleed seats to the players on the court. I wasn't going to let that stop me. I told him someday I would play in the NBA. Realizing that I had my mind set "Hoss" suggested that I transfer to Southern University in Baton Rouge where they played an up-tempo game that could benefit from my style of play. Little did he know that Southern would be in my plans soon there after.

6

Chapter Four

Mr. Norman/ Life & Basketball

Psalm 32:8
"I will instruct you and teach you in the way you should go; I will counsel you and watch over you."

My daddy had taught me to work hard and be honest in my dealings, and from about the time I was ten years old I worked in the summers for Norman Chenevert at the Crescent Plywood Company. Mr. Norman was one of the most instrumental men in my life. Crescent Plywood was where my daddy bought all of his materials for the jobs he was doing. Mr. Norman was incredible. He didn't have much education, but yet he started his own business from the ground up. He was a hard working man! We had a great relationship.

Mr. Norman poured life into my life. When business was slow we'd go into his office and have talks. His office was our little sanctuary. We'd talk about working hard and why it's important to work hard. We talked about his upbringing, too, because he too came from a poor background. Sometimes we' d talk about how he got started in his business. Starting from nothing he worked hard and grew his business. He encouraged me a lot. He instilled the work ethic in me. He even helped me buy a car. He followed my career through Southern University and on into the NBA. He kept my pictures in his office. He was a white man. He really treated me like a son. When I needed someone to talk to he was always there to listen along with my father.

I worked at Crescent in the summertime, and I worked hard. He really trusted me. I worked in the warehouse. I never gave his materials away. Guys would always try to get me to give them things. You know, an extra 2x4, stuff like that. He was a true mentor. I learned so many things from that man. He passed away in 2000. I basically saw him die. He had a massive stroke, so I left the Spurs to go visit him when he was really in bad shape. I was at the hospital when his son asked me to take a ride to his house to pick something up but when we got back a short time later they told us he had passed away. He was about 67 years old. His wife, Mrs. Joan, is a wonderful person too.

When I was just a little kid I had this ability . . . sometimes I wondered if it was a good thing or a bad thing . . . to talk. I could talk myself out of almost any trouble that I got into. Not that I got into a lot of trouble—I knew my daddy, Jim Johnson could give a real good spanking. But being able to talk was something that I was aware of. My mom, my dad, and almost any girl that I ever dated said I could talk the paint off the walls. Sometimes it worked, sometimes it didn't. I seemed to always be the guy taking charge.

Throughout my basketball career I've been called the "Little General" mostly by the players I played with and against, and some of my fans. Actually, how I got that name "Little General" was from Tom James, PR director for the Spurs. It was back when everyone was talking about Stockton and Malone the great pair from the Utah Jazz. You hardly heard one mentioned with out the other. It was always Stockton and Malone.

Now everybody knows that David Robinson is called "The

Admiral." I guess that's because he went to the Naval Academy. Tom said, "Stockton's got Malone so I guess The Admiral needs a General so we're going to call Avery "The Little General." Bam! The next thing you know they've got posters with me as "The Little General" on them all over and from then on people just started calling me "The Little General" and it stuck. Tom said it was because of my leadership and fieriness and stuff like that.

The leadership qualities I have to use in basketball are much like those used by a battlefield general, and they include having a grasp of what both my teammates and I can do. I know our strengths and weaknesses. I have to know the strengths and weaknesses of the opposition as well.

And that's how strategy comes in to play. It doesn't take much to figure out the strengths and weaknesses of the opposition, but it' s another thing to know how to successfully attack the weaknesses and stay away from the strengths.

The point guard has to be alert at all times. Things are moving fast, and play can change direction in a hurry, and there's no huddle and no regrouping after ever play. It's like a two-minute drill throughout the entire game.

It's the point guard's responsibility to know who's having a hot night getting the ball to go through the hoop and to get the ball to that player. He also has to know when to take the best shot available when the other players are having a tough time finding the hole.

I like the role of being in charge. I've always been a take-charge guy. It' s just the way I came into the world. Some people can hit a baseball like Mark McGwire or Barry Bonds, or skate like Sarah Hughes, some can box like Ali. Others, like Kurt Warner, can pass a football with nine hundred pounds of angry linemen charging them.

And it' s not only in sports. President George W. Bush is a born leader. Some can write like Tom Clancy, and others can act like Denzel Washington. These are just God given talents that the Creator gave to us when he brought us into the world.

(Jeremiah 1:5). I came into the world as a small package but God gave me abilities to lead and I've tried to do my best with those talents.

I think my first real experience with learning what leadership was all about happened when I attended Bell junior high school. I had a great basketball coach, Mr. Robertson. He was really mean and very serious. Nothing satisfied that man. He was a perfectionist. I remember sometimes having some of my best games, and yet that still didn't satisfy him. I feared that man. He scared the life out of me every day. But it was there that I started to understand what leadership was all about. He knew how to get the best out of you. He had a way about him. He had that special kind of voice. That voice was very intimidating even though he wasn't a big man. But he had a way of getting the best out of me because he put fear in me. It wasn't fear that I couldn't achieve, but a fear that made me want to achieve.

That's where I started to develop my toughness. With Coach Robertson I remember, starting to get tough. He showed me how to develop a purpose in my life as a basketball player. One day I got hurt but he made me play anyway. That helped me get tough. Today I love him to death, but back then I feared that man.

People ask me today what I think makes a good leader, and I tell them that in my mind leadership it is first setting an example yourself for those who follow you. On the basketball court I do that by working hard, coming early, leaving late. I watch a lot of film. I want to make sure I am always in the best shape possible. I actually work harder now than when I first came into the league.

Also another thing about leaders is that they develop other leaders. I didn't want to leave San Antonio without developing spiritual leadership in people along with basketball leadership. I think from a spiritual standpoint I enhanced the lives of Malik Rose, David Robinson, Monty Williams, Nick Van Excel, Calbert Cheaney, Ryan Bowen, James Posey and Antonio

Daniels. And I hope to do the same with my new Dallas teammates. I'm just talking about spiritual lessons, life' s lessons, and basketball lessons. Now those guys can lead in their own way.

Sometimes people are so selfish they don't know how to develop leaders. They're afraid that they will loose something by giving it to others. I believe that great leaders develop other leaders. (Moses developed Joshua. Paul developed Timothy. Lincoln developed Grant.) There are a number of players from the NBA that I admire as good leaders. John Stockton, Isaiah Thomas, Doc Rivers are some of them.

Avery kicking back in 1988

AJ in Florida 1989

Family & Friends in Golden State

Avery Relaxing

A.J., Cassandra and Christianne

Avery & Cassandra

Christianne at 8 months

Andrea,Christianne, AJ, and Inez Johnson (Mom)

A.J. and Mrs. Barbara (Merricks, A.J.'s Mother-in-law)

Captain Avery ready for a cruise

Christianne & Cassandra

Cassandra on Vacation

Chapter Five

Choices & Decisions

Proverbs 2:6
"For the Lord gives wisdom, and from His mouth come knowledge and understanding."

Making right choices is very important in life, and a lot goes into making the right choice, the right decision. Many factors enter into my decision – making process. I realized early on that making the right decision was important. I also had the love and input from wise parents. Even though they were poor financially and without much formal education they were rich in concern for their children.

I'm like everyone else. There could have been wrong choices that would have taken me down the wrong path. To stay away from the drugs and crime that so riddled the projects was a right decision. Choosing the right friends was one of the best things I ever did. When I was at Phyllis Wheatly Elementary school I hung with kids like Todd Millon and Eric Carr. They had the same interest as I, namely sports.

And you know God always seemed to send a person into my life to give me additional direction at just the time that I needed it most. And not only did I have good coaches, but they were also good people who cared about those that had been put in their charge.

There were coaches I've already mentioned like Coach Robertson at Bell Jr. High, Bernard Griffith at St. Aug, Ron Black at New Mexico JC, Ben Jobe and Tommy Green at Southern University, and in the NBA, Bernie Bickerstaff at Seattle, Don Nelson at Golden State and again with Dallas, Larry Brown, Bob Hill and Gregg Popovich at San Antonio, Dan Issel at Denver, Don Cheaney and Rudy Tomjanovich at Houston, all played an important part in helping me make sound decisions.

And from the time I committed my life to God in 1989 at the age of twenty-four I have called on the Master to guide my life and send people into my life that would be mentors that He would approve of.

Learning everything I could from Lujack and Joe Armant, both about basketball and life in general was one of the good decisions that I made early on. But playing point guard is all about making decisions. What play to run, who should get the ball, and how to get it to them. When to pass and when to shoot —those are all the decisions that are made at a fast pace, and they have to be made for forty-eight minutes every game.

Making decisions in life goes on 24-7. I don't want you all to think that I have made only right decisions, because I have made my share of wrong ones, but I have learned as I get older that sometimes God uses even poor decisions to teach us something, so I try my best to gain knowledge from my tests and trials. Making a right decision is getting easier for me. I like those bracelets, "What would Jesus do?" It's what goes into my mind–set. I need to think, "What would Jesus do?" What does God tell us is right in His Word?

I also think about what the consequences will be if I make a wrong decision. In fact, there's a lot that goes through my mind before I make a decision. I think that because sin is in the world it causes people to make wrong decisions. Lust and pride do that, and one big thing that happens a lot is that we want to be accepted. We want to have certain friends and run with the crowd. And then one big thing . . . we can be deceived. God talks about this in Isaiah, about the fact that what looks good can be wrong.

And again in Romans chapter 7, verses 15 and 16 Paul says, "I do not understand what I do. For what I want to do I do not, but what I hate I do. And if I do what I do not want to do, I agree that the law is good." He goes on in this chapter to tell of the quandary we all live in.

When I get to a spot where I need to make a decision and I don't quite know which way to go I tend to pray on it. I want to hear from God. I try to reflect on mistakes I've seen others make and I reflect on the times when I' ve made mistakes. And sometimes I still make wrong decisions. Sometimes I look to the men of the Bible. Abraham made a lot of mistakes, but God still called him a man of faith.

So even in my imperfections God still counts me a man of faith and a man of integrity. I fall short sometimes, but when I fall God is there to help me up, and I try not to make the same mistakes over and over again.

I'm like Joseph in the Old Testament. He went through some terrible tests. He had to *reach beyond the break* many times. He was sold into slavery by his brothers! You know that had to hurt. Then while doing a great job for his master he got falsely accused of doing something that he didn't do, and then he was thrown into prison for a number of years. But in all that God was with him each step of the way, and in the end he was second in command to Pharaoh of Egypt and helped save his people.

My dad was a leader. My dad could talk too. He was involved in probably ninety percent of my games. I remember him coming to my games right from work. He was exhausted, sweaty, dirty, but he still made my day because I knew he cared. He had to *reach beyond the break* his entire life.

In my New Orleans neighborhood my dad was kinda like a

dad for a bunch of kids. In the projects not many kids had fathers. But because my dad had left his kids behind in his first marriage he wanted to help these kids that didn't have fathers. I think he felt by helping these kids it was a bit of atonement for the past. So my dad was like a substitute father to them. He would talk and listen with those that had problems and he was always encouraging them. He' d tell them, "We don't know why your dad left. We don't know why things happen. So all we can do is live the best we know how." He'd tell them, "Don't hate your dad because you don't know all the circumstances why this happened."

When we played baseball he was always bringing a bunch of kids home, and my momma would feed them, or, other times he would take them all to McDonalds and buy them Happy Meals. And it wasn't just his kids but the whole bunch. Because I was playing sports there were always a lot of kids hanging around.

My dad was a church going man who loved God. He was a strong man—mentally tough. Man, was he a father! Though he messed up his first marriage with his kids, he more than made up for it with us. I can't speak for the other kids but to me he was a great example.

My parents loved their church. Second Zion Baptist Church in New Orleans was the first church I attended. My first remembrance of church was that it was long! I'd go to Sunday school and then the main church service and that' s what seemed long. Sometimes it was three and a half to four hours long. They'd be humming and moaning in there. I would be lying if I said I enjoyed church when I was young. I'm glad now that my parents made me go because I' m sure there are things that stuck in my mind and heart that at the time I didn't think were important.

I liked going on Easter Sunday the best though. They'd have an early sunrise service where they served food. I can still smell those grits cooking. The other good thing about Easter was I knew that even though it started at 6AM it had to be over by eight to start serving breakfast.

I have a total of nine brothers and sisters. My dad had six kids from his first marriage and my mom had two, then with Andrea and me that was ten. Their names are Cleveland, Lynn, Wayne, Cheryl, Andre, Edward, Patricia, and Rudy. I pray for them all the time.

I'm closest to Andréa. She lives in New Orleans and is a Principal Analyst for the City of New Orleans. She handles the personnel section for the utilities department. It's a very responsible job. We speak on the phone about once a week and sometimes we talk for a long time.

Family has always been an important part of my life and I am thankful for the family that God placed me with.

Avery now with the Dallas Mavericks shoots a foul shot against the Portland Trailblazers at the Rose Garden in Portland, OR.NBAE/Getty Images

Chapter Six

State Champions

Ecclesiastes 3:12
"I know there is nothing better for men to be happy and do good while they live."

I had a lot of fun playing basketball for "Hoss" and at Bell Junior High School, but now it was time for me to go on to high school. I wanted to attend Broker T. Washington High School because my friends in the projects would be going there but my dad had other ideas. He wanted me to get an education with a challenging curriculum.

The school my dad had in mind was St. Augustine, a Catholic boys high school that was founded fifty years ago for African-American young men.

When I first arrived at St. Aug, Watson Jones was the varsity head coach and Coach Bernard Griffith was an assistant. Coach Griffith is now the head coach there. In my sophomore year Terry Saulny was my JV coach. He gave me a chance at the starting point guard position and I did pretty well in high school basketball until my junior year. But I just wasn't ready. I ended up riding the bench all that year.

Watson Jones was the head coach of our championship team at St. Aug. Actually, Watson didn't like me as much as coach Griffith did, but what I remember about Coach Jones was that he was sort of like the general manager and Coach Griffith was the real coach.

Watson was murdered. He was just in the wrong place at the wrong time. Some people were looking for someone else in his family and they shot Watson by mistake. He was a kind man, an easy—going man. He didn't have a mean bone in his body. Coach Griffith, though, was hard as nails. They really balanced each other out very well.

Coach Griffith was mean, mean, just mean and disciplined, but he got the best out of you. When I say Coach Griffith was mean I guess I should say he was strict. He could make you run until your tongue fell off. He was a defensive guy, and he was all about discipline. Coach Jones was about being on time, but with Coach Griffith, if the ball was on the floor you better dive for the ball—you better dive for the ball or he'd take you out of the game. He was a no-nonsense coach.

In my opinion, (and if you ask other coaches they'll tell you the same thing I'm about to tell you) He's the greatest coach. . . he's the greatest coach in the history of high school basketball in the state of Louisiana.

I still see him all the time and I love that man. I work with the kids at St. Aug. I provide scholarships for those that need some help. He calls me a lot and we do a lot of stuff that doesn't get any print. I just want to give back a little of what's been given to me.

I loved high school. Those were some of the best days of my life as I look back on my time at St. Aug. The discipline, the camaraderie, the relationships that I built were great. They pushed you at St. Aug and I liked that. I liked the challenge. The struggle of handling something—then learning it—was great. The girls from the all-girls Catholic school loved us too and that was okay. I met my first girlfriend while I was at St. Aug. We dated for four or five years. Her name was Rachel Davis.

Playing baseball in high school was fun too. I'd go right from playing basketball to playing baseball. And it was around that time that I met Derek Lafayette. As the years went by Derek would prove to be my "friend of friends." We played together on the JV basketball team and that was the start of a relationship that has lasted to this very day. I guess we were about fifteen when we first met. I tease him some by telling him he doesn't have an athletic bone in his body.

Derek is not only my best friend. He helps me in many other ways. He's my assistant that handles many of my personal appearances and he runs my basketball camps. But there was a time in Derek's life when he just didn't seem able to keep from making some wrong decisions that made his life miserable.

He started fooling with drugs when he was in about the ninth grade. At first it was just marijuana. I shouldn't have said "just marijuana" because that's what most people think when they decide to use drugs.

It wasn't that Derek came from a bad family that didn't care about him. He had loving, caring Christian parents and he had friends that cared about him like me. Yes, he came from the projects but that wasn't an excuse for bad decisions. He went to St. Aug and was a good student but he made the wrong decision that day he decided to try marijuana. It went down hill from there. The drugs got stronger and stronger. He had to steal to pay for a habit. He was in bad shape.

I tried over the years to talk him off drugs but it didn't do any good at that time. Finally, one time about six months before I got married I went over to Derek's place and walked in and said, "Man, you better get yourself in shape if you want to be a friend of mine." God had been working on him and I guess when I told him what I did it was enough to make him call on God and ask for help in putting his life together. And God is faithful. Derek has been clean now for over ten years and will be receiving his BA degree in a few semesters. He is also licensed to preach and wants his life to count for God.

When we let God get involved in our decision-making the results are always good. There's no need to go it alone when you have the Creator of the Universe just waiting to help you.

I'll tell you more about Derek later but I've got to tell you this funny story about us while we were at St. Aug.

One time at the start of our senior year we decided we didn't want to take the regular math course so we went and begged the principal to allow us to switch to a trigonometry class that was being taken by a special junior class that was made up of smart, gifted kids. I mean real smart. He didn't want to let us take the class because he said it would be awfully hard, but we continued to beg him. He said we could take it when we got to college. But we kept on pleading, and he finally put us in the class.

To make a long story short: we got into the class and we were lost! We didn't know nothing! We were just lost! Mr. Carl Blouin was our teacher. We took our first test . . . at St. Aug. it' s customary for the teacher to call out the grades . . . he was calling out all these smart kid' s grades. William Becknell 90. Carlos Garcia 95 . . . He went down the line with all these kids getting ninety this and ninety that. Then he called Derek Lafayette, 40. I was laughing because I knew I had at least a seventy-five. Then he called my name . . . Avery Johnson. He didn't call my grade, he just handed me the paper. I looked and I got a twenty-two!

Derek and I knew we were in trouble and had to do something and do it quick—so we hired a tutor. We hired a young lady who tutored us the rest of the year. That was going to require some money, something that we didn't have a lot of. What we did was sneak out to the racetrack and play the horses. We also went to the pool hall and shoot pool for money. I was one of the best pool players in the neighborhood. Every Saturday morning and even sometimes after school I used to go there and play for money. And I could win a lot of money, a lot for then. That's where we got our money. Derek wasn't very good at shooting pool but he sure could pick the racehorses.

That class about drove us crazy. We couldn't figure it out. But as time went on and with the help we were getting we started getting better and better. By the end of the class we pulled out a C. That was the hardest C I ever earned in my life, but Mr. Blouin was so proud of us. Then my first year at New Mexico JC I had Trig again and man, it was easy!

Another funny thing happened while I was on the JVs. Lester Love, a friend of mine and a teammate couldn't catch my passes, so I made him carry my books home from school. Here he was about 6'2" and I'm 5'1" and he was afraid of me. I was feisty in those days though. Today Lester is the Pastor of the Greater Antioch Baptist Church in New Orleans where Derek attends.

Back to basketball at St. Aug: That junior year is one I would just as soon forget. I just wasn't ready. I was small anyway and this was some great team. There were many times that I felt like throwing in the towel. The reason I didn't quit when things were going that bad at St. Aug was because of my dad. I didn't want to let him down. Up to that point basketball had come easy for me, but I wasn't ready for the move up. I was smaller than the other players, and I wasn't really developed. My confidence was down. I was just 5'1" when I was a freshman and only 5'3" when I graduated.

That junior year was just another time I had to *reach beyond the break*. I had to take what I had learned from Coach Robertson and Coach Griffith and keep on going. It was very hard. When I wasn't playing people would make fun of me. I was the last man on the totem pole but I wasn't going to let down all those people that had believed in me but I really did want to quit.

But I stayed ready for the chance to play that would come. One of the hardest adjustments was that from the time I started at the NORD I was always the best. Now I was riding the bench.

We were called the Purple Knights and the team we had my senior year was one of the best teams ever to come out of Louisiana. We went 35-0 and won the state championship. No team had ever gone undefeated before. That year I was a much improved player, or at least Coach Griffith thought so, but we had so many great players that I didn't get a lot of playing time.

Donald Royal and Dwayne Lewis were the players the scouts from colleges came to see. Donald Royal went to Notre Dame, then to the NBA where he played for about ten years.

That year, the 1982-83 season, I didn't get to play a lot but I did play a little. It was just that Eric Williams was the starter, and he was really good, and his backup was Eric Coleman who was 6'3". All throughout that year I came off the bench, and I was afraid I wasn't getting enough playing time to attract any college scouts – and I really needed a scholarship to go to college. Without a scholarship I would have to go to USL.

It seemed my two last years at St. Aug I was always *reaching beyond the break* as far as basketball was concerned. But finally, I did get my chance just as the state playoffs were about to start. The starting point guard got into some trouble, I don't know just what, but anyway Coach Griffith came up to me and said, "Avery, you're going to play. You're going to be our starting point guard." I was as nervous as . . . I don't know what.

We started off playing a team in the city of New Orleans and won. Then we went out in the country to play South Terrebonne and won again. I remember that game because I made probably the best behind-the-back pass that I' ve ever made to Dwayne Lewis. I didn't score a lot. I was an assist man like Magic Johnson. They called me "Baby Magic." My friend Randy Ramie gave me that name. Now he calls me "Big Money."

Back then just as now I wasn't a big scorer. I was the point man on the defense and I was the point guard on the offense. When the team went flat, then I scored. When somebody else was going hot I got them the ball. I just did whatever it took for us to win. Of course to go through a season 35 and 0 is really hard, but the last five games were the playoff games, and they were harder than any of the other games because if you lost you went home. We were ranked fifth in the country.

We won the State Championship and I ended up being selected as the MVP of the playoffs and I was sure that would be enough to get the college scouts interested in me, but I didn't get one offer.

I used to think Coach Griffith was the meanest coach I ever played for, but he has been one man in my life that I could count on when I needed some good advice. Even after we won the state championship and I had played well it seemed like my basketball days were numbered. But Coach Griffith wasn't about to let me get off that easy.

In a 1990 game AJ moves the ball up court. Steve DiPaola/AllSport

Chapter Seven

Culture Shock

James 1:5
"If any of you lacks wisdom, he should ask God,
who gives generously to all without finding fault,
and it will be given to him."

I thought I'd probably go to USL (University of Southwest Louisiana.) I had been accepted there and I figured that at least I could get my education and get a good job. Then Coach Griffith introduced me to Coach Ron Black from New Mexico JC.

I was invited to a showcase along with several other players where we could show what we could do in front of the college scouts. Coach Griffith had invited Coach Black down to take a look at me.

Coach Black was really looking for a much taller guard or maybe a big forward but he liked my style and offered me a full scholarship right there on the spot. That was another time that I had to *reach beyond the break* mentally. I took Coach Black home to meet my family and they were convinced that he would do right by me. I accepted right there on the spot and was about to learn what "Culture Shock" was all about.

New Mexico JC is located in Hobbs, New Mexico It's a town of about 35,000 people. The closest big cities are about one hundred miles away. In New Orleans we had about seventy percent black people and in Hobbs there was about six percent. I never saw so many white people before in my life.

That flight in August of 1983 on Southwest Airlines was my first airplane ride. We made a stop in Houston and then flew to Midland, Texas. It was exciting. From that time on I knew that was the way I wanted to travel. Over the years I did encounter a few flights that could have changed my thinking about flying. One time flying from Houston to San Antonio it got so rough with turbulence and all that I thought it might be the end! The lady next to me was throwing up and the plane was bouncing around, but we made it, and even though I've had other rough flights I still love to fly.

New Mexico JC had a great reputation in the JC ranks and produced some quality teams. They played in about the best JC conference in the country at that time. But I have to admit going to Hobbs, New Mexico gave me mixed emotions.

Hobbs is down in the very southeastern part of New Mexico. Besides all the white people, I'd never seen red dirt before. (It was clay) The culture was so different even in little things – like when other people ate potatoes, I' d eat rice. And snow! We went up to Amarillo, Texas to play a game, and when we got there it was snowing and it was freezing cold. I didn't want to get off the bus. It was just total culture shock.

I think because of my personality I had a fairly easy time adjusting to it. I was pretty mature for my age and Coach Black was a great man. He was a real role model for me. He made sure my needs were met as much as he could.

I had a great year there. It was my first year in college and playing college basketball. The biggest problem there at the school was that we didn't have any transportation and the dorms were about three miles from the main campus, so we had to hitch hike to school.

One morning . . . I've got to stop here and give an explanation so things won't be taken the wrong way. At this time I was not a committed Christian and I drank some. I wasn't a drunk but my first two years in college I was a severe drinker. That lasted pretty much until my rookie year in the NBA, at which time I decided I couldn't live with one foot in the church and the other in the world.

Anyway, one particular morning I was a little hung over and wanted to get the first ride to school that I could. So along came a big long black hearse. The driver stopped and told me to hop in back. So I got in back and there was a casket there. And these were weird looking people. That was the longest three-mile ride in my life. When he let me out of the hearse I sprinted to practice. I ran across campus so fast I'm sure I broke a record of some sort and my hangover was cleared up.

My year at New Mexico JC was a wonderful experience. Coach Black is a man that I will always respect and I will always appreciate all that he did for me while I was there. I didn't come into college with a big reputation like some of the other players there so I had to really work hard. There was another point guard they had from New Orleans that I was battling for the starting position but I won out and was the starter.

My stats were not that great but okay. I averaged about 6 points a game along with 7 assists. Coach Black always said. "You can't judge your point guard on how many points he scores."

Just before Christmas I got hurt. I came down after making an easy lay- up and hurt my hip. I actually pulled the muscle away from the bone, and that could have been the end of my basketball career. Thank God we were at Christmas break when it happened and we had a month off and plenty of time to mend. I was able to come back and play though not to the best of my ability.

It was at this time that I was getting calls from Ulyen Coleman, who I knew from high school. He was now up at Cameron University in Lawton, Oklahoma, and he was telling me I should come up there, that it was a nice place.

Well I have to admit that the living conditions at New Mexico JC weren't that good. The transportation was bad, and the food service was not what I had hoped for. On the weekends we were pretty much left to fend for ourselves. If it were not for Coach Black coming by and picking me up every Sunday to go eat at Furr's Cafeteria I probably would have starved.

All those things and the fact that I was getting an offer to a four-year school appealed to me. I wasn't sure just how things would turn out after the first year at New Mexico. That hip injury was on my mind. I thought, *"What if I get hurt again here? Then what?"* I knew it would be hard to work and go to school and get my degree, and here was a scholarship looking me in the face that would guarantee me an education if all else went bad.

I talked to Coach Black about it, and he was super about the whole thing. I knew he would have liked me to stay and play for him but on the other hand he' s the kind of man that thinks not just of himself but the future of his players. He probably could have talked me into staying pretty easily, and now, looking back on how things turned out I wished he had. But then again, it was part of the plan to make my story more powerful.

In the end I transferred up to Cameron, and it was a bad experience from start to finish. Every night I would start to go to the pay phone to call Coach Black to come and get me but then I'd just turn and head back to my room.

I had run into racial problems previously, but nothing quite like it was at Cameron. It was very subtle. I'll give you an example. I had an accounting class and I'd go in for tutoring and the conversation would go something like this:

"Excuse me sir, I really don't understand this."

"What is it you don't understand?"

"I just don't get it. Could you kinda break it down for me?"

"There's nothing to break down. There's nothing to explain. What it is, is what it is."

This could go on for an hour like that, and finally I figured it out – he really doesn't want to help me. And with basketball I' m not one to toot my own horn, but I was ten times better that the kid starting at point guard. But the coach was just not going let me play. Racial prejudice is sometimes very subtle. In restaurants the service can be terrible if you are black. Just little things like that.

That year I watched Southern University loose to St. John's on television in the NCAA tournament and I thought that was awesome. Here they were from Baton Rouge, Louisiana, and they were a black college. It was all very exciting, and I wanted to be part of it.

I knew I could play there so I called up my old high school coach, Coach Griffith, who was at that time an assistant at Southern working with his old college coach Bob Hopkins. I told him about my situation at Cameron. It was on Easter Sunday of 1985 and I said, "Coach, I'm in a bad situation and can't get tutored, and the coach here doesn't want me to play even though I'm ten times better than the starting point guard. I'm having a hard time academically, and the professors are driving me out of my mind up here. I saw you guys lose to St. John's in the NCAA tournament. I would love to come back home and sit out a year and play my last two years at Southern. Can you help me out?"

I knew if Coach Griffith wasn't able to help me, it was all over for me as far as basketball was concerned. But Coach Griffith helped me *reach beyond the break*. He said, "You know, you can quit or you can *reach beyond the break* and give it one more chance and come down here to Southern University."

I said, "Coach, you know that's a good idea." Coach Griffith helped me more than once to *reach beyond the break*.

Chapter Eight

Coach Jobe & Ant Man

Jeremiah 29:11
" 'For I know the plans I have for you,' declares the Lord, 'plans to prosper you and not to harm you, plans to give you hope and a future.' "

Within three days Coach Griffith had an application in the mail to me and I signed with Southern and went down to Baton Rogue. I felt great. I felt like I was getting a new lease on life. Once more I was *reaching beyond the break.*

Transferring to Southern in Baton Rouge was like a home coming. I would be near my family and friends and even if only for a short while I was reunited with my high school coach Bernard Griffith.

I knew this was going to be a big jump up, but I was ready for it, and the confidence that Coach Griffith had in me gave me that little extra. Southern University plays in the Southwest Athletic Conference (SWAC) made up of Alcorn State, Grambling State, Mississippi Valley State, Alabama A&M, Alabama State, Jackson State, Prairie View A&M, Texas Southern, Arkansas Pine-Bluff and The Southern University

Jaguars. That conference produces more professional athletes than any conference its size in the country.

I'll tell you a funny story. My dad said, "Son, when you get to Southern University you go and find the two women on campus that confirm the cliché' " beauty is more than skin deep." They will be your two cousins." He told me one works in the cafeteria and the other works cleaning the dorms. So I got to the cafeteria and looked for the woman, and I found her. I went up to her and said, "Mam, my name's Avery Johnson, I'm Jim Johnson's son."

Her name was Delphine. She just went wild! She started saying, "Oh my cousin, oh my cousin, I'm so glad you are here. I'll take care of you." So to make a long story short: I never had to stand in line for my food. She always gave me more than anyone else. Then on Sunday's, after I got out of church I'd go to her house to eat. I did that for the three years that I was at Southern.

Delphine and her sister Nancy, kept putting confidence in me. They were always encouraging me. They'd say I was going to be something special! Or they'd say, "Boy you're great! Boy we love you!"

They had a little hole in the wall house right off the back of the campus. Those cousins took good care of me. They'd say, "Boy, we didn't graduate from college or nothing but you . . . you are something special. Boy you' re going to be in the NBA! Boy you can do anything you want to. You might be a preacher. They'd just go on, and on and on. They instilled a lot of confidence in me. Those two ladies had a big influence on my life and I love them so much.

Soon after I got to Southern Coach Griffith left to go back and take the head coaching job at St. Aug. The year I had to sit out at Southern was actually a great year. I remember the first day on campus I was in the dorm when a guy named Craig Pollard came into my room. He' s probably the meanest player that I ever played with, pro or college. He was 6'7" and a real intimidating looking guy. He was the headman on our press. He was real scary looking. Spit would be coming out of his mouth. Blood would be coming out of his mouth. He said to me, "What are you doing here?"

I said, "I'm here to play basketball. I'm sitting out. I'm a red shirt."

He replied, "You ain't playing basketball for us!"

Now here's a giant who just came from the NCAA tournament and here I am this little . . . "Yeah, I'm little but I can play."

He said, "We'll see about that. Meet us back of the campus this afternoon. We'll see what you've got." I thought they were going to let me play. I thought they were going to let me get out on the court and show them what I could do.

That afternoon I went to the back of the campus where they had what they called "free play" but they would never pick me on their team. I was going there for a month straight and they never picked me. They just wouldn't allow me to play. I felt like a Bad News Bears player or something. When he said meet us at the back of the campus and we'll see what you' ve got I thought I was going to be able to go back there and show them all my stuff, all the new stuff I'd been working on. But when they wouldn't let me play it made me feel, it made me feel . . . like I was garbage. It was like I was just trash.

Finally I said, "Man, when you going to let me play?"

He said, "You can't play with us. We don't like boys from New Orleans anyway." Stuff like that. Then one day Coach Hopkins came by and said we were going to have a game with the red shirts playing against the varsity. Now he had two all—Americans and two all SWAC guards on the varsity. We played them two times and I think I scored thirty points against them both times.

From that time on it was, "Boy, we didn't know you could play like that *Ant Man.*" That was my new nickname *Ant Man.* After that my name got out and people started treating me differently. Girls started treating me differently and people all over the campus and in the classroom treated me differently too. Even the most important, guys on the team treated me differently. The coach even allowed me to travel to some of the away games with the team. Coach Hopkins told me, "Avery, I need you right now."

When Coach Hopkins resigned to take the Head Coaching job at Grambling State he tried to get me to go with him. I was working my usual summer job at Crescent Plywood, and he called me every day to try to get me to go to Grambling, but I wouldn't leave Southern.

My next coach at Southern is one of the best basketball coaches in America right now. His name is Ben Jobe. He's an older man, in his late sixties, and he had me for two years at Southern. I learned so much from this man. He mentored me about the game of life as well as about basketball. He fathered me, he taught me, and it was a great experience.

Ben Jobe had been one of the outstanding coaches in Jaguar history going 193-101 in ten years at the helm. This would be his second tour of duty at Southern. He had coached at several other schools. The very first team he ever coached was Cameron High School and they won 24 games and that's still a school record.

Coach Jobe has always been a teacher of fundamentals, and during a five-year stint at South Carolina State College he produced five NAIA playoff teams, including teams in the finals in 1970 and 1973. The South Carolina House of Representatives commended him with a resolution of his achievements on the court.

He loves Southern University. He's been quoted as saying. "SU is hallowed ground to me. It holds a very special place for me. I believe if you can't win here, you can't win anywhere."

I remember the first time I met Coach Jobe. I came into his office and he asked if he could help me. I told him I was a basketball player and he said something like, "I believe that may be suspect."

I think he wondered a little about me. I had already been to two colleges and this was my third. I knew he had that running through his mind. He said that he liked a point guard that can shoot, a point guard that can score. I told him that was going to be difficult because I'm more of a passer. He told me to just work on my game and get in shape.

Coach Jobe was a well traveled man. He had been a lot of places and some of them were very impressive places. He even spent some time in the NBA. When he was coaching at South Carolina he took his team to the finals of the NAIA a couple of times. He was even honored on the floor of the House of Representatives in South Carolina with a resolution because of his contribution to basketball. He was some man and some coach.

My junior year we went 19-12. We won the SWAC Tournament and I was named SWAC tournament MVP. I also led the nation in assists that year. We lost to Temple in the first round of the NCAA at the Rosemont Horizon outside of Chicago. That loss wasn't that devastating. We were just over matched. We played our best but they were just too much for us.

But after that season I knew I could play at the Division I level. My confidence was sky high. It was just soaring! I was MVP of the SWAC Tournament and I had led the nation in assists. Things were finally going my way. I was really looking forward to the next year and was still working on my game, trying to improve, trying to get better. I wanted to get stronger, get quicker. My confidence couldn't have been better. I had proved to myself and to others that I was a legitimate Division I player.

My senior year we went 26-7. It was just an outstanding team. There were some great players. Four of the starting five graduated, thanks to Coach Jobe and Coach Tommy Green. That year I was SWAC player of the year and again led the nation in assists. We went to the NCAA tournament again but were beaten by Kentucky. They were just too big and too strong for us. They dominated the game inside, but it was a great experience playing there with the best players in the country. Rex Chapman the all-American from Kentucky came up to me after the game and told me he admired my game. That made me feel real good!

I have a friend from that team who is playing overseas now. His name is Kevin Florent. He was my best friend on the team. He's playing in Greece now and he's been playing over there for fourteen years. Another guy on that team was Derwyn Johnson. He was one of the best shooters I've ever seen, and Derrick Anderson came off the bench. He' s a good friend of mine. Bobby Phills who passed away tragically last year in a car accident was a freshman on that team and he went on to play in the NBA. A couple of other guys were Carlos Sample and Slim Goody. We had some solid players. At that time we were probably the best small college team in the country.

I enjoyed going to school at Southern, even though it was hard. There were some really tough professors. One who comes to mind was Dr. Kessler. She worked me very hard in psychology, but even so I got my degree in psychology in May of 1988. It was an awesome experience for me. We had a lot of fun there, but it was clean fun! They pushed us academically. And we had some great games against some big time universities.

I met my wife there right after I graduated. Kevin Florent introduced me to Cassandra. She was in nursing school and I had had my eye on her for some time. Her maiden name is Merricks. Kevin came over to my place and said, "Avery, I' ve got someone I want you to meet." So he took me over to Cassandra's apartment and introduced us. Like I said I had been watching her most of the semester outside the nursing building. She was not a basketball fan and never heard of me, but we hit it off. She's a big fan now and knows the game as well as I do.

Another exciting time for me was when I was privileged to

be the one blessed to see my parents take their first airplane ride. We went to New York City of all places. After my senior year at Southern I was taken to the NIT Tournament to be honored at halftime for leading the nation in assists.

When we flew to New York my dad was so nervous. He probably smoked ten packs of cigarettes. That was back when you could smoke on airplanes. We stayed at the Marriott Marquis Hotel. It was funny because my dad asked, "How much is it going to be for food and stuff?"

The concierge said, "Mr. Johnson, you have a master account. You can order drinks, room service or whatever you want."

My parents were just scared. They hardly came out of the hotel. They just ordered room service. My dad and I took a walk for about two blocks, and then he was ready to go back to the hotel. I don't think my mom ever left the hotel except to go to the game. The game was at Madison Square Garden, and at half-time they gave me a trophy. My parents were so happy and proud. We stayed in New York for another day before we flew home.

Chapter Nine

Congratulations Rook

Proverbs 15:30
"A cheerful look brings joy to the heart, and good news gives health in the bones."

I just knew I'd be drafted by an NBA team! You couldn't have convinced me that I wouldn' t. I had the college record for the most assists for one year with 13.3 per game. I was averaging 11 points per game. Here I was one of the best players in the country and I didn't get drafted. I really took it hard when that happened.

I was down in Florida playing in the United States Basketball League at the time of the draft. I watched the draft on TV with my friend Kevin Florent and I was sure I was going to be picked in at least the second round. They had three rounds back then. When I wasn't taken in the third round I was really down. Here I was again finding it necessary to *reach beyond the break*. I was beginning to wonder what I had to do to get a break.

That was one of the most dejecting periods in my life. There was no way in the world that you were going to tell me that Avery Johnson wasn't going to get drafted. There's no way! No way in the world! You're telling me that I' m not as good as seventy-eight other players in the country. When that third round ended and the last pick was called I just turned the TV off.

Kevin was with me to celebrate what we were sure would be me getting drafted and starting my NBA career. It was terrible but then an hour later my phone rang and it was the Seattle Super Sonics inviting me to come to their rookie camp. I also got calls that day from the Atlanta Hawks and the Golden State Warriors with the same offer. I was down but now I felt like I at least had a chance. Do I just stand there holding a broken rope or do I *reach beyond the break* and say let me go to this summer league?

During my senior year the NBA scouts were at all my games and a lot of my practices. I thought maybe the Indiana Pacers would take me. Mel Daniels was their scout at the time, and he used to come to watch me a lot. Coach Jobe was a friend of Donnie Walsh the GM at Indiana, but that didn't happen.

I decided on Seattle. I went to rookie camp in July of 1988 for one week. I was battling for one spot on the team against Cory Gaines, a point guard out of Loyola—Marymount, he came in with a lot of hype about the fast break he ran in college. They drafted him in the third round.

We worked out for a week in Seattle and then went and played in the Pacific Northwest Review in Portland. I thought I played well there. That was my first time playing against Terry Porter. Then we went down and played in Los Angeles in the summer league. That' s where I made my name. I was the best point guard in the league and we had a great team.

After that I went back to Seattle where Coach Bernie Bickerstaff of the Sonics offered me a partially guaranteed contract. He gave me ten thousand dollars up front. Bob Whitsitt was the general manager then (now he' s at Portland). I knew if I came in and worked as hard as I did in the summer league I would make the team, and that's kind of what happened.

Cory Gaines, Ricky Winslow, and I used to have breakfast in the hotel restaurant. As the pre-season started to wind down, more and more guys were being cut. Then it was getting close to the final cut, and John Lucas, Cory, Ricky and I were all eating breakfast. After breakfast we usually got a cab to take us to practice. So we headed for the cab and it was just John Lucas and myself. John said to the driver, "Let's go."

I said, "Hold on John, we can't go yet. Ricky and Cory are still in there."

"Let's Go!"

He answered me something like this. "Shut up young fellow. The axe is falling." I really didn't know what he meant, so finally, when we got to practice I started counting. I was going one, two, three, four and so on, and then I said to myself, " *There's only twelve people here.*"

Then Bernie blew his whistle. We were standing at half court. He said, "Congratulations young fellow, you made the team." I was so excited I started running around the gym. I was the happiest man on the face of the earth. All the guys were rubbing my head, patting me on the back saying, "Congratulations Rook!" Just hearing that was one of the most incredible things that ever happened to me. My first contract with Seattle was for one hundred thousand dollars. After my first year with the Sonics they resigned me to a one-year deal for a guarantee of two hundred seventy five thousand dollars

It was at the end of my first year in the NBA that I decided to follow Jesus. I had been *reaching beyond the break* all my life even though I didn't know the saying. The day I was baptized was the day I really decided to follow the Lord. I had been in and out of the church. I had one foot in the church and one foot in the world most of my life. I was good at going to the night clubs on Saturday night and even drinking up the whole bar, then getting up and going to church on Sunday morning. That day in July, the day I was baptized, I was out until 5:30 in the morning in New Orleans on Bourbon Street.

Drinking, drinking, drinking! I had six Michelob's, and six Long Island Ice Teas, and six shots of whiskey so I was out of my mind, and sure hadn't planned on going to church that morning. I don't even know how I got home. At 10:15 in the morning I felt as if there was a tap on my shoulder telling me to go to church. I could barely open my eyes. I got up and got dressed, still hung over, and I went to church.

Bishop Paul S. Morton of the Greater St. Stephens Baptist Church was preaching a sermon called "Fully Committed." It felt like it was just Bishop Morton and me in the church at that time. Nobody else was there, and he said, "Some of you out there have one foot in the church and one foot in the world. Today is the day for you to become fully committed—not partially committed, but fully committed to Jesus.

Something welled up in me as if the Holy Spirit was taking control of me. Bishop Morton hadn't finished his sermon before I began walking up to the front to give my life to Christ.

So I gave my life to the Lord that morning, said the sinner's prayer, and went home. My dad was lying on the sofa. I could not even get the words out of my mouth to tell my dad what had happened before my dad said, "I already know."

I said, "You don't even have an idea what I'm about to tell you."

He said, "I already know."

I wanted to tell him that I was getting baptized that night at six o'clock but dad said, "I'll be there at six."

It was a couple of years before I really felt comfortable sharing the Word. I was just trying to figure things out my first couple of years as a Christian. To help me understand better I started to spend more time around Christian people and I think God just started transforming my mind. That helped me quite a bit. He was dealing with me in a way that made me more conscious of sin. I was more conscious of bad choices, not only in big things, but in little things too. (You know how we are. "That was just a little lie. Things like that.") I became more conscious of how the world was and of the sin in the world.

I also became more stable in my relationship with my wife.

God has given man domain and he pretty much sets the tone in the family. As I became closer to God, I became a better man and started growing in my faith. And it stabilized my relationship with my wife as well.

I began speaking at a lot of smaller functions like little father's day luncheons, and things like that, where people really didn't know my name. Then, as time went on, I even found myself preaching in front of forty thousand people. On that occasion I was with Franklin Graham, Billy Graham' s son, in Amarillo, Texas. That was exciting! I had never talked in front of that many people before. I was just in awe that God, the Creator of the Universe, would use a little man from the projects. That He would think enough of me to put me on Franklin Graham's heart to put me in front of forty thousand people! Obviously I had sinned many times. I had done some things before that God didn't like, but He would still think enough of me that I would have a word to tell those people.

Working with my foundation in San Antonio laid the groundwork for a lot of the later success that I've received.

Seeing the transformation in my best friend' s life really showed me the power of God. Derek finally decided to let God have His way in his life and that was about the time I became fully committed also. Derek started praying and attending NA meetings regularly. He was fully committed to getting off drugs and getting his life cleaned up for the sake of all those people he felt he had been letting down.

Three years ago my agent, Tony Dutt, hired him as an executive assistant.

Chapter Ten

Released

II Corinthians 1:4
"Praise be to the God and Father of our Lord Jesus Christ, the Father of compassion and the God of all comfort, who comforts us in all our troubles, so that we can comfort those in any trouble with the comfort we ourselves have received from God."

One thing that helped me get along in the NBA was that I knew how to serve people. I think I probably learned that from my momma. I' ve never been jealous of people. Even though Nate McMillan was my rival as the starting point guard I worked with him. Whatever he wanted me to do, I did it. I've never been envious or jealous of anyone else' s game. I was so appreciative at making the team. I just waited my turn.

I was in Seattle for two great years. It was unbelievable! I was a reserve and learned a lot from John Lucas who I would later team up with when be became the coach at San Antonio. Nate helped me in many ways too. They used to call me the Tasmanian -Devil, because when I got on the floor I used to be all over the place. Dale Ellis and Xavier McDaniel were the ones that tagged me with that name. They made it "Taz" for short.

A strange thing happened in my second year. The Sonics

drafted a young boy right out of high school named Shawn Kemp. That was interesting because back then that just didn't happen every day. Shawn was a super athlete, and has had a good career in the league. We now also have the same agent, Tony Dutt.

Tony Dutt was another man who has been very instrumental in my professional career. We've been through a lot together. There were moments when I wanted to fire Tony. It wasn't his fault my career was a roller coaster. I think we have one of the best player-agent relationships in all of professional sports.

Tony is not a perfect man but he has worked to get me the contracts I've had. He's beat down doors for me. There have been times when I've talked to him forty times in one day trying to get a deal. And he would seldom have any good news for me, but he'd hang in there. We got these free cruises through the NBA, and when I'd get home from a cruise the first person I' d call was Tony Dutt. Even when the news was not good he would always put a positive spin on it. When we didn't have an offer he was always confident, always confident! This man, more than any other player or coach in the NBA believed in me. Tony Dutt convinced Bob Bass to give me a shot in San Antonio. I love Tony Dutt.

I had a great time in Seattle. It was a great town. The people were very good to me. It will always be one of my favorite places. I'll always be thankful that I got my start there.

After my second year Bernie Bickerstaff left the Sonics and took the general managers' job with the Denver Nuggets, and he traded for me in November of 1990. Denver picked up my contract. I was only in Denver a short while, and then I got cut. I'll always remember that. It hadn't happened to me before, and they gave me the word on Christmas Eve. What timing! They told me as I was standing outside the locker room in Portland where we had just played. I had to fly back to Denver with the team and that was awkward to say the least.

I was so down in the dumps that I felt like going out and

drinking all night long. I felt like going out and drinking a fifth of Crown Royal. It caught me so off guard. I felt like I had been blind—sided. It was like my heart literally dropped to the floor. I think the first time something like that happens to you, especially something that bad, the sting is a lot harder.

I thought there for a bit that my career as a basketball player could possibly be over. I didn't know about going and trying to get picked up by some other team. I realized it is tough to make it in the NBA especially for a point guard who hasn't played much. I thought Cassandra wouldn't love me anymore. I thought now that I was cut from the NBA is she still going to want to marry me?

My dad was the first person I called. He told me, "Son, come on home. Come and be with us at Christmas." I really needed that from him.

Then when I got back to the hotel I called Cassandra and gave her the news. We were engaged at the time. She said, "Come on home." She told me she loved me. She picked me up at the airport on Christmas Eve. I cried like a baby. I sure didn't feel like it, but I knew I had to *reach beyond the break* again.

I sat out for about two weeks and then San Antonio signed me for the rest of the season for the league minimum of one hundred forty thousand dollars. It so happened that just two weeks prior to that I had fifteen assists against the Spurs while I was at Denver. They needed a backup for Rod Strickland so it worked out well.

Cassandra ended up moving to San Antonio, and she got a job at Methodist Hospital. She worked twelve-hour shifts four days a week. We moved into a nice little high- rise. We were waiting to be married that summer.

Chapter Eleven

Gladness and Sadness

Psalm116:15
"Precious in the sight of the Lord is the death of His saints."

Psalm 118:29
"Give thanks to the Lord, for He is good;
His love endures forever."

We got married that summer on July 6, 1991. We were married in the same church that I was baptized in, Greater St. Stephens Baptist Church, and Bishop Morton conducted the ceremony. He was the pastor who preached the "Fully Committed" sermon that changed my life.

It was a big wedding with over four hundred people attending. There were eight or nine bridesmaids and grooms men. My best man was my brother Edward. My mother-in-law Barbara Merricks was there. She' s a wonderful person. We hit it off the first time we met.

The night before the wedding we went to visit my dad in the hospital. He didn't look too good to me but he assured us that he would make it to the wedding and he did.

Coming to America is my all-time favorite movie and we took a scene from the movie where we had little girls dance down the isle before Cassandra. I told her I always wanted a wedding like that.

It was a beautiful wedding. We had a big Rolls-Royce limo and the whole works. The only thing that wasn't that good was the weather. It was rainy and windy. But other than the weather it was great. We had wonderful reception at The Southern Plantation. A few of my NBA friends were there. David Robinson came down. Michael Adams, Derek McKey, Olden Polynice, Morton Wiley, Tony Massenburg, they all were there.

Cassandra was really nervous. But me . . . I wasn't nervous. Right! I was so nervous that if it hadn't been for Lester Love I think I would have gone out the back door of the church. My tux was all messed up and he helped me get that straight. He gave me a handkerchief just in case I had to wipe my eyes. It was a good thing Lester was there.

The next morning we had our first argument because Cassandra couldn't find her birth certificate and here we are scrambling around at 5:30 in the morning and were exhausted. We' re trying to get to Jamaica for our honeymoon. She thought she had put it in one place and then the other. We were right down to the wire to leave on our honeymoon but thankfully we found it.

We spent about five days in Jamaica. It was really nice. We stayed in a place called The Sandals. It was an all-inclusive resort. Just a great place! It was warm and sunny and the water was warm and crystal clear. We went to a place called Dunn River's Falls. It was a big waterfall with rocks you could climb up.

We also took a bus to Ocho Rios and had a great time there. There were nice hotels and great dinners where my wife and I could just sit and talk like honeymooners.

I had to come back and play in a summer camp with the Spurs. So we came back to San Antonio.

I started that next year with the Spurs. Rod Strickland was holding out, and they needed me. But once again it seemed to happen to me at the worst time—the Spurs cut me. I had just gotten back from David Robinson's wedding where I was a groom's man when they called me and told me I was cut.

When they cut me, of all the people who could have called me on the phone to tell me about it, they had Pop do it. Larry Brown had him do it! Pop wanted to come by my house, and so I asked him why he wanted to come to my house. He said he just wanted to come over and talk to Cassandra and me.

He said, "I feel real bad about this."

I said, "Pop, it's hard for me to go from going to one of my best friends wedding and then you cut me. Why did they cut me? There is no reason. Even if Rod Strickland is coming back you need a back up. I mean they just cut me. Bob Bass cut me!"

I was told it was about the salary cap. And here I was finally getting some stability in my career. I' m here in a city where people love me. . . . It was funny. The day after I got cut I was in a Wal-Mart store and I probably signed more autographs in that store than I did in my entire stay in San Antonio. They had all heard my interview on TV. The day I was cut all the television stations had cameras out to my house and I did an interview in my front yard. They were all asking me what I was going to do next. I told them,' When God closes one door He always opens another." Here was another time that I had to *reach beyond the break*. It just seemed like I was always reaching, reaching, reaching.

I sat out for three weeks. I sure was getting tired of *reaching beyond the break*! I had a little different thinking this time. I felt sure that somebody would pick me up. The first time I got cut I wasn't thinking like that. This time I thought I'd be picked up in three or four days and when that didn't happen it got a little rough.

After sitting out for three long weeks I signed with the Houston Rockets on a ten-day contract, then another ten- day contract. Two was all they could sign you for, and after that they had to sign you for the rest of the year or release you. So finally they signed me for the remainder of the season. It didn't hurt that I scored twenty-two points against Minnesota on the last night of the second ten—day. Unfortunately Don Chaney the coach that liked me got fired and Rudy Tomjanovich came in as the new coach.

I finished the year with the Rockets. At the end of the season I was what is called a restricted free agent. Houston traded and got Scotty Brooks and that made my job insecure to say the least. That meant I could be picked up by some other team but the Rockets had the right to match that deal. What happens is that teams think you are just using them to run up the salary with other teams. I wanted the Rockets to release me so I would be an unrestricted free agent and be able to sign with whoever I wanted for whatever amount I wanted. While I was a restricted free agent the Rockets had control over me, but they didn't have to pay me.

I was really angry that the Rockets wouldn't release me. I probably called Rudy Tomjanovich every bad name in the book. I was so mad! I said, "You don't want to guarantee me the money. You don't want me on the team. But then you don't want to give me my unconditional release."

I was angry, and my wife was angry. She was telling me to quit. She said, "Baby, you need to quit and go get a real job. You've got your degree. You'll be successful in whatever you try." I thought about it but I was just holding on. I had the broken rope in my hand again. But I kept on going to the gym. I kept on running and holding out hope and I kept reaching.

Rudy Tomjanovich told me he didn't like me. He didn't like my defense and didn't think I was much of a shooter. I said, "Rudy, in that case why don't you just release me?" They held onto my rights through the whole month of October. Then my dad died, and I don't know if they felt sorry for me or what? But after he died they released me.

I hadn't been in training camp with anyone. The rope was getting harder to hold on to all the time. My wife's pregnant, I'm out of work, we're having financial trouble, and then I got word my dad had passed away.

My father had had heart problems as long as I can remember. There were times when he was in the hospital and my mom didn't even want to tell me. The night before Cassandra and I were married he was in the hospital, and we weren't sure if he was going to be able to come to the wedding. Cassandra and I went to visit him in the hospital, though, and he was telling us not to worry that he'd make the wedding. And he did, even though he looked a little frail and weak—but he made it.

He was a chain smoker and a social drinker. And he didn't always eat right because in our culture we ate a lot of fried foods. Almost a year later when Cassandra was pregnant, I went to visit my dad in the hospital because he was in bad shape. He had suffered another heart attack or two so I went to see him and talk to him. He couldn't really talk too much. He said he was going to be all right—But He just didn't look right.

I had to go back to Houston. My wife was pregnant, and I had to work out because I was out of a job at that time. That was in between the Houston Rockets and my return to San Antonio. That same night when I got back home we got a call at about eleven o'clock from my brother Edward to tell me my dad had passed away. I talked to mom on the phone, and she was really hurting. Cassandra was totally upset too.

The next day I flew back to New Orleans and I pretty much had to take over the funeral arrangements. My dad had a little insurance but there were still things that had to be taken care of. The way I felt when my daddy passed on was that I was sure that I wouldn't be able to *reach beyond the* break, but with my mother's help and strength I did. I *reached beyond the break* and God pulled me safely to Him. It had just seemed like the reach was too far, but again the Lord was faithful, and He brought me strength through His Word and friends that He sent to help lift me up. It sure wasn't a great time for me.

I just know he's up there in heaven looking down on me and smiling. He's probably got a bunch of kids around him playing ball. I know there will be basketball in heaven and I'm sure I'll be seven-foot three and have moves like Michael

Jordan. Wouldn't that be something!

There are still nights before games when I think about my dad, but he kind of programmed me for the time when he would move on. When I was growing up he would tell me that it was fine for me to think about him after he passed away, but he' d also say, "I just want you always to be better than me. That's all I want you to do, just be better than me in every area of your life." He'd tell me not to get all—emotional when he went on. Don't use me to get up for some game. You should get up for the game because you love the game.

One of the fondest memories of my dad was from a time when I was in the third grade. He bought me my first pair of Dr. J shoes. There really wasn't any money for extra things. But one day my dad walked into my room and said, "I' ve got a surprise for you." He busted out a pair of Dr. J's. I knew we couldn't afford them but he was proud of me— proud of what I had accomplished—and he wanted to let me know. He said, "I believe in you and you believe in me and I want to reward you with these basketball shoes."

My dad taught me pretty everything I know. He taught me how to be a man. He taught me how to be a husband. He taught me how to be a hard worker. He taught me to take pride in everything I' m involved in. He taught me how to follow instructions and listen carefully. Even though I talk a lot I try to be a good listener.

I had played part of that year with the Spurs and part with the Rockets, but my spending was out of control. What was happening was that my bills were continuing to come but my paychecks had stopped. I was spending more than was coming in. My salary wasn't that good at that time anyway. It seemed like everything was coming down on me.

Chapter Twelve

SA to Golden State to SA

Job 42:2
"I know that You can do all things;
no plans of Yours can be thwarted."

Here it was October and I hadn't been to training camp with anyone. Then the Spurs called and wanted me to come back. Jerry Tarkanian was the coach at the time. He hated me! He loves me now but he hated me then. He wanted Gary Grant who was making one point two million dollars at that time with the Clippers. He was saying that if Avery Johnson is that good why doesn't he have a job. He didn't understand that you could be a good player but with rosters being filled, you could be the odd man out on a particular team. He didn't comprehend that. The "Shark" valued being a good NBA player by how much money you made and not how you played. He got fired about two weeks after I got there. But he wrote me a great letter two years later and told me how much he loved me and was sorry for what happened.

John Lucas came in as coach and he made me a starter at San Antonio. It felt incredible! I was on top of the world. Just on top of the world knowing I was running the show. I knew everyday when I came to the arena I was going to be in the starting lineup. That was just incredible! I had known John from Seattle and when he put me in the starting lineup I was as high as I was low when I was cut in Denver. It was good to know that the first time you messed up you weren't going to be taken out of the game. It gave me a lot of confidence.

We had a great year. We lost to the Phoenix Suns in the second round of the playoffs when Charles Barkley made one of his unbelievable shots, but it was still a great year.

After the season the Spurs didn't want to resign me. I couldn't believe it! I just knew my time had come to get a multi-year contract with some decent money. Again I sat out all of October. I couldn't get any other team to sign me, but then, finally, Golden State called me. Tim Hardaway had blown out his ACL playing in a preseason game up in North Dakota.

Gregg Popovich was an assistant coach with the Warriors at that time, and he called me from a phone on the airplane and said they were looking at me. He said they were looking at Steve Kerr and a couple of other guys. "I' m trying to get Don Nelson to sign you," he said. So he convinced Don Nelson to sign me—probably after a few beers (Ha! Ha!) I signed a one-year guaranteed contract for three hundred thousand dollars and an option for a second year. This time the option was mine.

I had an awesome year! I was named Captain of the team after only being with them for nine days. I started 72 out of 82 games. I averaged more points that year—somewhere near ten points a game. I had a career high for minutes played with 2332. We had a great team with players like Chris Mullin, Chris Gatling, Billy Owens, Latrell Sprewell who was first team all-NBA and Chris Webber who was Rookie of the Year. It was Don Nelson who encouraged me to start shooting the hook shot. He said he thought I had the best hook shot of any guard in the league. That put confidence in me there. I really liked Golden State, but at the same time going back to San Antonio was exciting too.

After we got swept by Phoenix in the playoffs, Pop told me that if the San Antonio Spurs lost to Utah something was going down. So the Spurs ended up loosing to the Jazz and Pop got the General Managers job in San Antonio. He asked me to opt out from Golden State and come to San Antonio and I'd be his starting point guard.

The move from Golden State was a little sad, though, because Coach Nelson gave me my first opportunity to be the starting guard for the whole year. It was fun playing with the Warriors. But that's the way things happened—I signed a three-year contract with the Spurs. It was my first long—term contract.

I was feeling great! Cassandra was feeling great! This was my first multi-year contract with decent money. The Spurs held a big press conference. That was the first press conference I ever had. My mom was there and my little daughter Christanna was a little over one and a half. We were all just so excited.

Because we had wanted to build a home in Houston we thought this was our dream coming to pass. It was just great with all the excitement in being welcomed back. The fans were excited because they knew the Spurs needed a point guard. Everyone was excited because they had seen me climbing, climbing, climbing up the ladder. I was finally getting some respect and it felt good! It was welcome back AJ. AJ is our guy. AJ is a Spur. Man, that felt great!

The team had Pop back along with Sean Elliott and Chuck Person. I was back with the Spurs for the third time. We were moving in the right direction to have a championship team.

That year got off to a rough start. Chris Whitney, one of the guys backing me up, really embarrassed me in training camp. He was running circles around me. Coach Bob Hill was asking me. "Don't you want to be my point guard? Chris Whitney is killing you!" Chris is now playing with the Washington Wizards and he calls me his mentor.

I was never one to have great training camps anyway. Then one night it all came together in Mexico City, Mexico. We were playing the Houston Rockets. I mean I caught fire. It was a five—alarm fire. I think I had something like 24 points and 12 assists. Coach Hill said, "Okay, now I see what I've got." Then the next night I played well against Seattle. So from that point on Bob Hill had a lot of confidence in me.

But the regular season started off with us struggling. Oh were we struggling! We were 9-11 in our first twenty games. Here we thought we had a championship team and we're struggling. No one could tell me we weren't a championship team.

But we just couldn't find the groove. We just couldn't get on a good winning streak. Our defense was just okay. We were trying to figure each other out. Dennis Rodman was on the team. Sean was trying to get it together. I was trying to do my thing. Vinny Del Negro was the two—guard. I had a lot of fun playing with him. He was a bright guy, well educated from North Carolina State. I probably achieved more playing with Mario "Junk Yard Dog" Ellie but I had the most fun playing with Vinny because physically we didn't scare anybody.

We spent a lot of time together doing all sorts of things. We did a lot of charity work in the San Antonio area and we were able to help raise a lot of money for needy projects. If he put his mind to it Vinny could be a pro golfer.

But we just couldn't get in a good groove. Then one night it all just came together. In Houston Texas against the Rockets we played a great game, and from then on we didn't look back. We were one of the deepest teams in the NBA. It was one of the best teams I've ever played on. Our second team was really great, including Doc Rivers, Willie Anderson, J.R. Reid, Terry Cummings and Chuck Person.

We finished 62-20. Man we went on a crazy run. We won 51 games and lost just 9 on that run. That was the best record in the NBA that year. It was just an exciting year. I couldn't wait to go to the arena for a game. I averaged 13.1 and 7.9 assists. I recorded 20 assists twice that year, once against the Los Angeles Clippers and again against the then Vancouver Grizzlies. It was a great year. That' s when the Little General and all that stuff got started. I was named to the NBA All-Interview team for the first time and was named winner of the 1997-98 NBA Sportsmanship Award. That' s one honor I cherish. The NBA donated $20,000 to St. Aug and $5,000 to Sam Houston HS in San Antonio in my name for getting this award and that really made me happy.

We added Doc Rivers to our team at the beginning of the year, which gave us another veteran guard. Doc was great to work with, and he was solid down the stretch. Doc' s now the head coach of the Orlando Magic. David had a great year. He was the NBA MVP. We were a great team that went to the playoffs. We were the number one seed since we had the best record in the NBA.

I think we swept Denver in the first round then beat the Lakers 4-1 in the second round. But, then . . . here we go! In the Western Conference finals, playing against the Houston Rockets . . .We probably had beaten them seven out of eight times we played them that year including pre-season games . . . and here we go. In the first game we lost to them. We lost to Houston in the first game on a game winner by Robert Horry because Dennis Rodman didn't want to rotate to him. So we lost to Houston in the first game.

Then in the second game of all things that could happen I sprained my ankle badly. Hakeem Olajuwon is destroying us! Now we go down 0-2 in the first two games before an average of 38,000 fans at our house—right there in the Alamo Dome! We had the home court advantage and still couldn't win!

I remember coming in afterwards, and we had this big meeting in the locker room where everybody was screaming at each other. Guys were cursing. We didn't even have practice that day, we were so mad at each other.

Moses Malone had one of the classic one—liners. He was

talking, talking, talking when I said, "You don't understand, Moses, you were good when you played." Then Moses said, "Man, I've been a bad basketball player since high school!" He used some different language in there but you get the meaning.

I think I got along well with Dennis Rodman. Jack Haley was his main man. I think that's why in his book he said I was one of the players he really respected. He said he didn't like it here, but I think he was jealous of David because David was making a lot of money and he wanted David to play tougher and all that.

So here we were down 0-2 against the Rockets. We didn't have practice, but that meeting got things turned around. After that meeting I went out and tried to run on my ankle. Paul Pressy kept telling me, "You've got to push it. You've got to push it. I know you're hurting but you've got to try and run on your ankle today so it will feel better tomorrow. If you don't run on it today and you try to run on it tomorrow it won't feel good."

My ankle was hurting! I was screaming in pain in the Alamo Dome, running up and down the court. He kept pushing me. "Come on Avery. Come on" Paul said to "Keep trying. Keep trying. You got to do it today." But the next two games my ankle was still hurting but I had to play on it.

The next two games we beat the Rockets in Houston, and they were two of my best games of the series. Now we were 2-2 and we came back to San Antonio before 40,000 people. And of all the things that could happen the day before the game, Dennis Rodman didn't show up for practice. That was just Dennis being Dennis! He liked the spotlight and the attention and this was one way for him to get it. As a team we were mad at him, but Dennis is Dennis. Then we decided not to start Dennis in game five. We were disciplining Dennis Rodman in the conference finals instead of disciplining him after the season with his contract. That was a mistake. We played right into their hands.

So we lost game five and went back to Houston and lost game six. And that was probably the worst I ever felt in a basketball season. I cried after it was over in the locker room. We could here them saying, "Tickets go on sale for the finals." I will never forget that! Never! We had put so much into that season, our team did. I thought all the time we were going to win a championship. And now I was heartbroken

Houston went on to win the NBA championship by beating the Orlando Magic.

Chapter Thirteen

"I Gotta Plan" –Tim Duncan

Psalm 94:17
"Unless the Lord had given me help,
I would soon have dwelt in the silence of death."

The off season wasn't as bad as I thought it might be. I had had a good season, maybe my best to date. But I did have a lot of sleepless nights. I saw us winning that championship. I thought we could win it. I was really angry with David. I was angry because he was the MVP and he didn't play like one. I think Hakeem played an outstanding series and made every play. I don't think I even called David in the off—season. I was really angry! Not because it was his fault. I'm a Christian and he's a Christian and he' s my friend. I just felt he could have played better but in hindsight Hakeem was just unstoppable.

We were getting ready to start the second season on my new contract in 1995-96. I knew this team wasn't going to be as good as last year's team. We traded Dennis Rodman to the Chicago Bulls for Will Perdue. Now Will' s a good player but we were trading away the best rebounder in NBA history. We still had a good team. We went 59-23. I had my best individual season ever, period! I think I finished second in the NBA with 9.6 assists. I averaged 13.6 points per game and an assist-to-turnover ration of 4.05-1, the best of any starter in the NBA. That was the best season for me as a pro, period!

And off the court we had a new addition to the Johnson family as Avery Jr. was born on July 12, 1995 and we moved into our new house in Houston.

We knew that we were going to have a baby boy after the sonograms but nothing could prepare me for the excitement I felt the first time I held little Avery Jr. Cassandra had some problems during this pregnancy and we had just finished what we thought was a dry run to the hospital and we were getting ready to go back home when my wife went into intense labor. It was a good thing we were at the hospital because he was ready to come out. He came into the world kicking and has been kicking ever sense.

I love both of my children equally but there is something special about having someone to carry on your family name. I'm carrying on the Johnson family name and that's a good feeling.

We had a good year. We won the Division. But we ended up loosing to the Utah Jazz in the second round of the playoffs 4-2. Utah was always a nemesis for us. I hated to play against John Stockton. I couldn't beat him to save my life.

I was feeling good. I was playing all-star caliber basketball. The fans were loving me! Everything was going well. Cassandra was happy!

But the third year of my contract was one of the most disappointing years that I have had in all the years I've played basketball. The team was awful. San Antonio players missed a total of 347 games through injury—by far the most in club history. David Robinson got hurt in my hometown of New Orleans against the Rockets and it was all down hill from there. David would end up missing the entire season.

Then Chuck Person got hurt. Sean Elliott was out all year. I had to sit down and that broke my consecutive games played at 378. Of all things I had an abscess on my throat and that' s what stopped my string. I was real proud of that. Bob Hill got fired. We brought in a thousand different players that year. We really did have 24 different starting lineups that year. We had some players on the team that year that were just totally selfish. That was just an abomination year. We only won twenty games. Also Kim Perrot, a good friend of mine lost her battle with cancer that year. She not only was a great basketball player for the Houston Comets of the WNBA, but she was a remarkable person who I miss very much.

Pop took over as coach. He was always telling me, "Don't worry. We're going to be okay. I gotta plan." He always had a plan. He'd take me to dinner and say, "Don't worry about it. I got a plan." I said I sure hope your plan is good.

I probably need to stop right here and say something about my relationship with Gregg Popovich. Gregg Popovich has probably had more to do with my over all success as a basketball player than any one in my career. He was responsible for me going to Golden State at a time when I really needed a job and that's where things really started to turn around for me.

Then he brought me to San Antonio as his starting point guard. He gave me more room to operate, more responsibility on the court than any coach I had ever had. I was into the game plan more with Pop. We had some great years together. And he' s super nice man. He's not fancy. He doesn't put on any airs. He's just Pop!

He has always been very nice to my family and I judge people on how they treat my family. I have traveled many miles with him and I know the kind of man he is and I can only say thanks to him. Thanks Pop!

It wasn't my worst year individually but it wasn't my best either. I felt badly about the loosing.

When we drafted Tim Duncan from Wake Forest University that was a happy day in the Johnson house. My wife was running around jumping and shouting. I was too. The kids were all jumping with excitement. They didn't even know why they were jumping and hollering. We're yelling, "Timmy! Timmy! We're back! We're back!" We were just excited.

That was the year that I followed David Robinson, my brother in Christ's leading and formed the Avery Johnson Foundation, and over the next several years we were able to give and to raise from others money for a number of needy charities in the San Antonio area. One of our main projects was working with a homeless-teenage pregnancy home called Seton House. That was our signature charity where I did all kinds of personal appearances raising money and I gave money out of my own account. There were a number of other charities like the 100 Club, which is a foundation for children of men and women killed in the line of duty. We gave a ton of money to the churches. We gave money to Respite-care, which is a home for physically challenged kids. We were able to help a number of groups in San Antonio

1999 was the year that my mother developed cancer. My sister Andréa never wants to worry me and tell me the whole story. By the time I got the true picture we found my mom had full-blown cancer. She had it everywhere. She had it on the breast, the stomach and on the brain.

She went through radiation and chemo treatment. I went home to see her. It was a sad sight. She had lost all of her hair. She was so frail looking from all that chemo. I just cried, I just cried but not in front of her.

She kept getting treatment. I came home for the summer and I took my mom to get some work on her arms because her veins were so small from all the treatments. They had to put this in so they could draw blood for all the treatment. It was a minor surgery. Then we came back home. My mom was so weak she couldn't pick up a glass.

Then I had to leave and go back home because my wife and I had planned a trip to Miami—Fishers Island—a nice resort area. This was in August of 99. When we got to Fishers Island the place just felt weird. There was something wrong with my spirit. I just couldn't get into it. We were supposed to be having fun but I couldn't?

We had barely got our bags unpacked when my sister called me on my cell phone. She was calling from my mother's home and said mom isn't breathing. Another very good friend from the neighborhood went to aid my sister, his name was Barry Stamps. Barry was another one of those good male influences on my life over the years. We used to go by his house every Saturday to eat dinner. He was just a good man. He always had a bunch of boys come to his house and eat and play basketball.

So Barry was there and he got on the phone and told me, "She's not responding. She's not responding." It was a terrible time. I felt so helpless. I was on the phone and Cassandra was crying and saying "Oh Lord, Please Lord." . . . Then she was gone.

We didn't sleep one second that night. We packed up our things and flew out on the first flight we could get which was at six in the morning. We got into New Orleans about eight am. My brother Edward drove in from Dallas. I had to make all the funeral arrangements. Everybody was so sad. Andrea had to get the clothes that we wanted mom to wear.

I don't have any fond memories of going back to Miami. It just brings back bad memories.

I'm glad I had a mother like I did. She was so involved in my life. After my dad died she came to a lot of our games. My mom would come to my foundation events and things like that. And when we had to move mom would come and help us. My mother-in-law, Barbara Merricks, is the grandma that plays with the kids and my mom was the one who cooked. They were a tag team.

Mom had been through so much. I knew that she was going to be at peace. No more suffering. She deserved that. My mom passed on August 13th in the home that I was able to buy for her after my first year in Seattle. I had a little money that I had saved, although my career was far from stable. But I made up my mind I wanted to do something for her before I did something for myself. I wanted to get her out of the projects so she wouldn't have to hear cursing, wouldn't have to worry about gun shots anymore.

Just to see the smile on her face when I got her that house was worth it. I was glad that she was at her home when the end came. My mom hated hospitals, as most people of her generation did. And she had been in and out of the hospitals a lot in her last months. I have to laugh when I think of mom giving me her funeral instructions. She said she didn't want a long funeral and she said, "Avery, make sure the Reverend doesn't go on and on." My mother was a psychologist without the sheepskin hanging on the wall. It will be great getting to heaven and seeing my mom and dad again. Praise the Lord!

Chapter Fourteen

World Champions

Psalm 19:5
". . . like a champion rejoicing to run his course."

That season was amazing! Man, it was like nobody could get to the basket on David and Tim. It was awesome! That year Tim came into training camp as the best player on the court. He was even better than David. David couldn't stop him. He was a nice kid, a mature kid for his age. He had a psychology degree. We just hit it off from the beginning. I mean he respected me, and what I do. It was just great.

Then we traded for Antonio Daniels in the off-season and that was good. I took him under my wing.

The season got off to a great start. Tim was playing up to expectations. Pop put in a defensive philosophy that was going to result in Tim blocking shots. Tim had an awesome year. I' m not sure whether we won the division or not. But the playoffs were another disappointment. Tim sprained his ankle in the second round. Again Stockton gave me fits, and it was just tough. We were still encouraged. That was a fun year. We all improved defensively. I think we were ready to head back to being a championship caliber team. But we were just missing something—toughness!

We started to get toughness when we brought in the veterans Jerome Kersey and Mario Ellie. That was the difference. Toughness . . . They had been there. Mario Ellie and Jerome Kersey had played on championship teams. I talked Pop into bringing Mario in. We were looking at a whole bunch of other players. Dale Ellis, Tracy Murray, and they were all shooters. I had played with Mario at Houston and I told Pop, we' ve got to get Mario Ellie, and as it worked out, he really helped us a lot.

This was going to be the shortest NBA season in history because of the strike. We got off to a slow start. I think we were 8 and 9. Boy, they were talking about firing Pop. I got really nervous. I remember we had a meeting at Pop' s house. Pop said, "Well guys, what are we going to do?" I gave him a few ideas. David gave him a few ideas, and boy, from that point we got rolling and didn't look back.

That strike season was tough. A lot of times you had to play three games in a row. You were always tired. And the waiting! The off-season ran all the way to February. It was tiring with all of the meetings and all of the talking. It was tough just trying to find stuff to do. There were a lot of long days and sleepless nights. You know, you wanted to play ball. We were coming into a season with a championship team. A lot of people predicted we'd win it all.

The 99-00 season had many highlights for me and my wife. I reached the five thousand career assists plateau on February 27, 2000 against the Minnesota Timber Wolves. Then with three assists on December the seventh I passed Johnny Moore as the Spurs all-time assist leader. And again I was picked for the NBA All-Interview team. Ha! Ha! My wife and I were so proud to be given the President's Award for service to Families by the Family Service Association. Getting the Most Caring athlete Award by USA Weekend touched my heart.

But when we turned it around we never looked back—never! We were getting tough. David and Mario were jawing at each other. But as it turned out, it made us tougher. We got into

Avery hits a jumper in game six to give the Spurs The NBA Championship against the New York Knicks at Madison Square Garden in 1999. Nathaniel S. Butler/NBAE/Getty Images

the first round and beat Minnesota. The second round we swept the Lakers. Then we swept Portland.

Damon Stoudamire, the Blazers point guard made a statement before that series that "San Antonio would never win a championship with Avery Johnson as their point guard." I don't make comments about other guys and I really don't care what comments they make about me. I said when this series is over we'll let the winning take care of any comments a guy has made. Damon and I talked briefly after the season. We cleaned things up a bit between us. Like I' ve said all along, whether Damon says anything good or bad about me, I like him. I like him because he's short and he's left-handed like me. He has a tough job leading a team as talented as the Blazers are. I' ve been in those situations, especially when things don't work out and a lot of fingers are pointing at you. He's in a tough position and my heart goes out to him. I just like him. After the game he told me just to keep proving people wrong.

We played the first two games in San Antonio at the Alamo Dome. We had swept through the playoffs so we had ten or twelve days off before we played again. The Knicks took a long time to get to the finals. They had a long tough series with the Indiana Pacers. It was a long time waiting and practicing and watching them play. That is just too long to be off.

We started out hot in what could be a seven game series. Tim had an incredible first game. He had close to 40 points. We went up on them 2-0. Then it was time to go to the Mecca of basketball, New York City, for the NBA championship. I can remember being in New York and having the fans cursing me out and saying, "You suck, Avery Johnson. You ain't going no where in New York. You are garbage. Charlie Ward is going to eat you alive. Sprewell is going to kill you, Avery Johnson!" They would throw beer and French fries on my wife. They were just doing all kinds of crazy stuff. Those are things you have to live with. You don't like it, but you have to live with it.

We lost game three because early foul trouble hurt us.

We ended up beating them in game four and then beat them in game five. Game five was one game in which I had to *reach beyond the break* because I had five or six turnovers at half-time. And when it came down the stretch they came to me and they got me the ball and the rest is history.

The score was Knicks 77 Spurs 76. That final play we had called a play called four-down. We're going to Tim. It' s no secret. Basically on four-down Sean Elliott starts under the basket and floats out to the wing and I give him the ball and he gets it to Tim Duncan. But for some reason Sean was denied. So I brought the ball to the wing. Sean Elliott took my place at the top of the key and then I threw the ball in to Tim. But when I threw the ball in to Tim Duncan, Sean Elliott' s man, Latrell Sprewell went to double team Tim. When he went to double team Tim Duncan, Tim threw the ball back out to Sean. My man, Chris Childs, left me and went to Sean Elliott thinking he was going to shoot the ball. Sean pump faked taking the shot. Then I slide down from the left wing to the left baseline He penetrated left. Latrell Sprewell ran and tried to block my shot, but the ball went in the hoop. Everything was going so fast! That ended up being the game winner. I had no hesitation about taking the shot, thanks a lot to my teammate Steve Kerr. He told me what to do if I got into that situation. He had told me that maybe six or seven months before. Steve had a similar situation where he took the winning shot to give the Chicago Bulls a championship a couple of years back. Steve and I have had similar careers and we both came into the NBA in 1988.

There still was forty seconds to go. Forty seconds seemed like a long time—**a** long time. They came down and took a shot and missed. Then we got the ball and did the same thing. Now they had the ball out with about 2.7 seconds to go on the shot clock. They inbounded the ball to Latrell Sprewell, and he missed the shot. That was one of the happiest moments in my entire life! I jumped on Sean Elliott and I almost broke his back. I was excited!

A lot of people came out on the court. The players were running everywhere, crying and screaming, shouting, our families were there Derek was there. It was just incredible.

I was trying to find my wife, and then she made her way out on the court and I kissed her. I was crying and she was crying. I can't begin to tell you how important my wife has been to me these past fourteen years. She has gone through thick and thin with me. Through being cut, being traded, through the deaths of my parents, to tell the truth I'm not sure how I would have done it all without her.

She is so easy to communicate with. So understanding. Her job is as close to a single mom's as you can get. When I'm on the road she has to do it all and she does it very well. Getting the kids to school outings, sports, piano lessons and the like, I don't know how she keeps up. I wanted her with me at this moment to share in the excitement.

It was awesome. It was just awesome winning the championship! We were on top of the world! We had tears of joy. I had said it before: "You're judged by the time you go somewhere you haven't been before, and I won't have proven myself until we win it all. Well, we won it all. They said we couldn't do it, but we did. We proved we could win the big one."

And you know what? It's not even just winning the championship that blows my mind. The thing that blows my mind is that I'm a starter. To hit the last shot of the Finals . . . that's what people are going to remember. I' ve been truly, truly blessed. Making that shot was also great because a lot of people, coaches—and a lot of teammates I've played with over the years have helped me a lot with my jump shot, which has always been an issue in my career. And I want everyone to feel good about it. Thank you all for helping me, and for believing in me!

You feel relieved when you come to a time like that. I remember we were celebrating in the restaurant and Peter Vessy was there and he bought us deserts. I told the guys, I will drink

Avery Says Peace

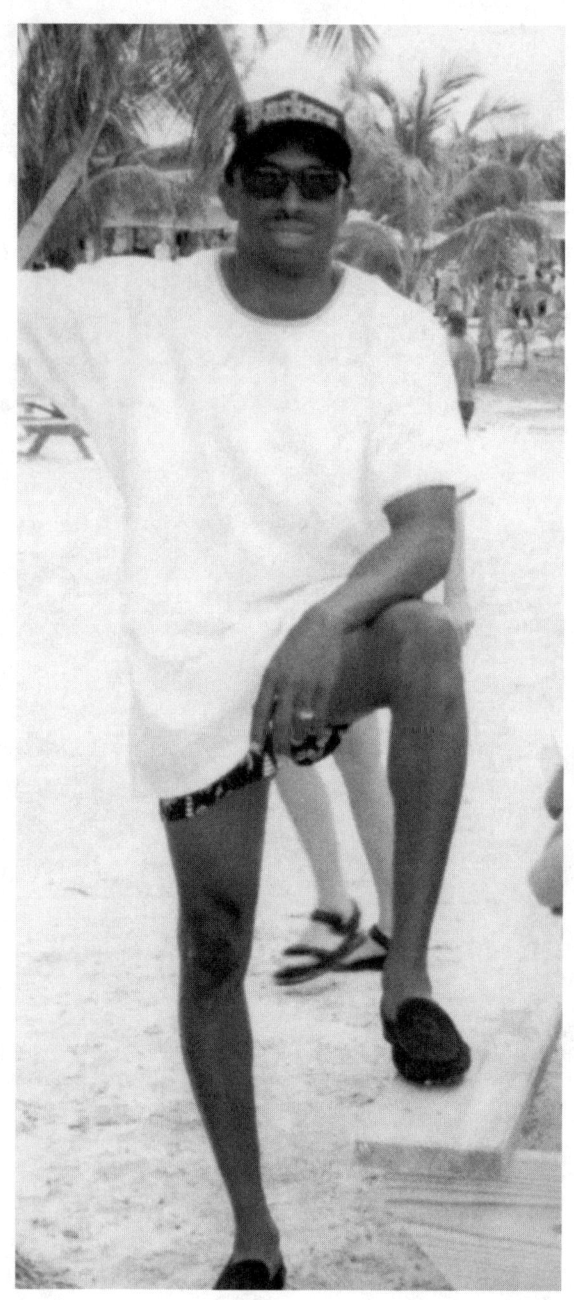

Avery - Great Legs

Avery & Christianne at one

Christianne, A.J., Mickey, and Cassandra

Avery and A.J. and one of the horses Derek picked

Cassandra, Avery Jr., Christianne, Avery

Christianne & Avery Jr.

Avery Jr., A.J., a friend and Christianne

Christianne, Avery and A.J. Jr.

Avery doing yard work

Coach Ron Black NMJC & Avery

Avery gets another assist at Southern 88

some champagne if we win the championship, but I' m not a drinker.

We were having fun. A bunch of my friends were there. Derek was there. Lamar Holt who I've spent a lot of time with spiritually, doing business, etc was there. Eric Bowens, and Derek Anderson my good friend from Baton Rouge were there. Derek is a long time-friend from college and he was also in my wedding. We were all at dinner. My wife and all my friends were there. We just had a great time.

Then when we got back to San Antonio that next day – wow! Oh my Gosh! All the people that were at the airport! David and I walked out of the airplane carrying the championship trophy first. There were thousands of people going crazy. Thousands, thousands!

Three hundred thousand people showed up for a parade along the River Walk. We all rode in these little riverboats. Then when we get to the Alamo Dome there were forty thousand screaming fans there. It was awesome! It was incredible! I can't even begin to tell you how I felt. And for the people of San Antonio it was a great time, too. This was their first championship too.

Later after winning the championship we went to the White House, and that was something! Just being in the White House and meeting President Clinton. Wow! And to think the Spurs organization thought enough of me to address the President was incredible. Meeting the members of his staff, seeing all the special rooms and the paintings on the walls could only remind you of the Presidents before like Abraham Lincoln and George Washington who had been right there, right where you were standing. The security there was unreal.

That off-season I was busy with personnel appearances. Maybe too many . . . I wore myself out. I was going everywhere.

I was doing a lot of speaking at church groups, corporate conferences, and at basketball camps. I was doing a lot of preaching. I was going a little bit of everything. I think the championship gave me an opening to go and preach and teach and witness like I had never had before. It really elevated my platform. Even though people may have a different belief—they may be Jewish, Muslim, etc. They respect hard work, consistency, integrity. Some people that I do business with are not Christians. It was like they might not have been ready to give their lives to Christ but my story is something that many people out there can relate to and being part of a World Championship Team was something they would get excited about and come out and hear what I had to say.

Chapter Fifteen

SA to Denver to Dallas

Proverbs 1:5
"Trust in the Lord with all your heart
and lean not on your own understanding."

I had one more year left on my contract as we started the next season. We had a tough year. We struggled. We fought against injury. I think I missed about six games that year with injuries. Sean Elliott was out all year when he had a kidney transplant. Will Perdue left to go to play with Portland. The last season was long and the summer was too short. Coming back as champions the pressure was on. It wasn't a let down. We just couldn't really get it going the way we wanted to. We thought we could win the championship again. I' m not sure whether we won the Division or not that year but I think we did.

I had one of the worst things happen to me as a player that year. I had a fight with Malik Rose. And I basically destroyed the locker room in Cleveland. I was under so much pressure. I was feeling like I was unappreciated by the Spurs. For the first time Pop and I got off track as a coach and a point guard. I felt like he wasn' t . . . there was something different about him and he felt there was something different about me. Malik said something to me during the game and I approached him after the game, a couple of punches were thrown. I was upset. I was in rage! We destroyed the locker room. I think we caused about five thousand dollars worth of damage. We did a little bit of everything. Thank God for Jerome Kersey because he held me back and if he hadn't Malik probably would have killed me. It was just an embarrassing situation and you're talking about reaching beyond the break. Malik had been in Bible study with me. And David was so mad with me, and wouldn't even look at me for a week or two. Pop wouldn' t look at me. I was embarrassed myself. It was the low point in my career. But you know a week or two later Malik and I talked it over.

Talking about reaching beyond the break . . . I had to reach beyond the break. Pop had to reach beyond the break. Pop was ready to trade me. He was ready to cut me. He was ready to just get rid of me. He was that mad. Then Pop forgave me. Malik forgave me. My teammates forgave me. I forgave myself and God forgave me.

Then when we got to the playoffs and Tim got hurt so we lost in the first round to Phoenix. I couldn' t really get going right. They benched me a couple of times in the fourth quarter, which was an unheard-of thing. I struggled a little bit because I think my head was a little big and I didn' t think Pop had as much confidence in me as he had the year before. It was just stuff! Just stuff! I don't think I was as approachable that year as I had been in the past. Things were just different.

The next season I signed a one - year deal for eight million dollars. I was one of the highest paid point guards in the league. They didn' t want to sign me to any longer contract. They said they had salary cap issues and things like that. So they ended up signing me to a one year deal.

It was pretty much an up and down year because I started off with a hamstring injury in training camp. I tried to come back but then really got messed up and I was out for about two months. Then when I came back Pop didn't put me in the line-up and I was disappointed about that. I felt like they gave away my job to Terry Porter. So I spent the rest of the year playing my role. But I never really got right. I could never feel good coming off the bench. You know, once you' ve been a starter it's hard to come off the bench. I thought I was the head of the snake and now they put me in the back.

We won the first and second rounds in the playoffs. Derek Anderson got hurt in the Dallas series. I was proud of the way Antonio Daniels, my man stepped up. Antonio and I went to lunch on almost every road trip. He's special to me!

We got embarrassed in the Western Conference Finals against the Los Angeles Lakers. Things just ended up on a sour note.

I was still holding out some hope that things would work out in San Antonio, but then when Denver came up with an opportunity I couldn't pass it up. They offered me a three- year contract.

The people from the Denver Nuggets were great. They took my wife and I all over town for three days. We visited some of the finest homes in the area, schools, churches and restaurants. All during the time in Denver I was hoping that their offer would be one that I could accept. It was going to take a heck of an offer to get me leave San Antonio. It would have to be a three-year deal or something like that.

Denver said that I was their number one free agent priority even before the last season had ended. They wanted to bring me in to back up Nick Van Exel as well as tutor the rookies. For me to be able at this age to command this type of respect from another team is just thrilling. They gave me a three year deal for . . .? HA! Thank God for Dan Issel.

So we took the deal and moved to Denver. Denver has great restaurants. We found a good school for the kids. Purchased a nice house in a great golfing community, Castle Pines and the season was going well. I knew this team was not going to be a contender right away, but it did have some potential. I was able to have an impact on some of their players. I've worked on helping some of the younger players with their games. Mike Evans took over as interim coach after Dan Issel resigned. I was looking forward to working with Dan but it didn't work out.

The team was awful. Bad chemistry, injuries, no confidence, you name it. I got off to a good start, and when Nick got hurt my playing time increased. I was scoring well and the assists were there. For me it was a matter of integrity. It was one thing when I was playing with the Spurs and we won the title by fifteen games, but it' s another to put it all on the line when you' re on a four, five or six game losing streak consistently and you know your team is really not even going to make the playoffs. To me, playing the same is what a professional does. I want to show those same qualities in either situation.

I love the city of Denver, and it was a great experience for us after living in Texas and some other places. Denver is in a beautiful part of the country.

I miss the relationships that I had developed over the years in San Antonio with the owners, coaches, and my teammates. I miss the Spurs staff. I missed the media. I had a great role model, Bob Brown. I had a partnership with the biggest bank in South Texas, IBC. Dennis Nixon, Tom Travis and Jorge Hayes are great people and friends. And I miss the fans. I had my critics, but I always thought 95 percent of the Spurs fans respected what we did.

In San Antonio I had the better of two worlds. I got to play on a great team like the Spurs in a wonderful city where people appreciated what I did in basketball and in the community.

I got a chance to work with Pastor Walker of Antioch Baptist Church on his project to build a Christian Life Center. They have a great ministry and do a lot of work on the east side. At that time my church home was in Houston at Brentwood

Baptist. Pastor Ratliff gave me my first chance to share a word on Sundays and it opened up future opportunities and I' ll always be grateful for that. I visited a number of outstanding ministries in San Antonio, like Macedonia Baptist Church and Pastor Jerry Daly. I got a chance to visit New Creation Church, with Pastors David and Claudette Copeland and Cornerstone Church with Pastor John Hagee who has one of the top ministries in the world.

San Antonio had some great golf courses but I have to admit I'm a terrible golfer. But I love the game. I hit a mean driver but the rest of my game is bad! Bad!

Denver made the trade with the Dallas Mavericks I couldn't believe it. I was on the way to take Avery to get a hair cut when Tony Dutt called me and said "You're going to Dallas." I was in total shock! Nick Van Exel, Raef LaFrentz, Tariq Abdul-Wahad and me, all going to Dallas. Now Dallas was probably one of the top four teams in the NBA and sure to be in the playoffs so when the dust had settled I was happy. Real happy!

Even though my short stay in Denver had been a good one it was good to be going back to Texas. I sure was leaving Denver with better feelings this time than I did when I was cut before by the Nuggets in 1990 with an engagement ring in my pocket.

Chapter Sixteen

This and That

Proverbs 16:7
"When a man's ways are pleasing to the Lord,
he makes even his enemies live at peace with him."

My off-season keeps me busy. With keeping in shape and making appearances it' s a hustle. I have some basketball camps in New Orleans, Laredo, San Antonio and in Buffalo, New York. Lamar Holt who I mentioned previously helped me in the beginning with basketball camps and he did an outstanding job.

A normal day in the summer goes something like this. I get up about seven and have breakfast. Then I go and meet my trainer, Leroy Franklin at the Sweet Water Country club. He has been helping me for a number of years. I work out with Leroy for about two hours. We do some weights and agility drills. Leroy is a big part of my success. Then I go eat a light snack. I have a protein shake. Mrs. Donna at the club makes the best shake in America.

Then I go to the West Side Tennis Club where John Lucas holds workouts. The tennis club is owned by Jim and Linda MacInvale. They have been so gracious to have let us (`NBA players) use their faculties for years. I even get a free lunch there! Jim is known as "Mattress Mac." He owns one of the biggest furniture stores in the country. I work out there from about eleven to one playing basketball. I eat that free lunch and take a break. We come back again and play beginning around five.

I do that four days a week. I take Friday off. I don't do anything. For conditioning I do a lot of bike riding, running on the track, tread mill, swimming. I mix all that into my workouts.

People ask me all the time to pick my all–star team of the best players in the NBA. Now that's hard to do because there have been so many great players, but I' ll try to give you my all-star team that I either played with or against.

At center I would take Shaq even though I'm biased towards David Robinson. Shaw in one word is "unbelievable." At one forward I' d take Larry Bird. Larry was the key to all those great Boston Celtic teams in the past. He could beat you so many ways.

I would have to take Tim Duncan as my power forward. He's only been in the league for a short time, but I think many people agree that he is probably the best right now and he has a lot of years a head of him. My point guard would be Magic Johnson of the Lakers. At six foot nine, he had moves like a player at six one. If his career had not been cut short he would have pushed Michael for the best player of all time.

That brings us to shooting guard and there is only one like this one - Michael Jordan. He was just unbelievable. He could do it all and a lot of people don' t realize he was a great defensive player too. When I was asked what I thought of him after playing against him for the first time I said, "He sure isn't overrated."

I had to leave some great players off that team, players like Isaiah Thomas, Karl Malone, John Stockton, Chris Webber, Patrick Ewing, Jason Kidd, Charles Barkley, and so many more.

Now if you think your team is better than mine make sure your players know how to reach beyond the break.

I've been asked if I talk much trash and I have to say no, I don't do much, but a couple of guys that could talk trash are

Gary Payton and Larry Bird. Now Larry was a quiet trash talker. He just sort of mumbled, just enough to play with your mind, whereas Gary could be heard by everyone in the gym!

I'm often asked what we do on the road. When we are on the road we do our Bible study about an hour before shoot around. We usually go no about twenty minutes or thirty minutes. I' m always reading things that I think will be interesting and beneficial, something that will be relevant to us. I try to do series studies. I might do a two-part study on temptation to let them know the negatives about temptation and how we can overcome temptation. I may do a Bible study on a particular book in the Bible like Philippians. I may talk about relationships. I've done a Bible study on prayer. I' ve done a Bible study on "Who is Jesus?" I've done a Bible study on loving your enemies. I' ve done a Bible study on confidence. You know, on having Godly confidence. David Robinson and I started doing that in San Antonio and I carried that over to Denver. There are a few guys who are serious about getting into the Word.

Everyone is not a believer but we don't care, it' s there for anyone who wants to come. We don't impose it on anybody, but guys hear about it and want to come. They're welcome to come. I did the same thing in Dallas and you could see guys mature in a short time. One thing about Coach Pop – he was were kind enough to let those of us who were spiritual, be spiritual. We prayed in the tunnel before every game with the Spurs. We had a fellowship night with the fans where we could preach the gospel.

I've tried to keep up my relationships with guys but it is hard. I'm on the other side and the side I'm on gets all of me.

There's a guy I grew up with named Randy Ramie, who was my best friend for a number of years early on in life. Now we might talk three or four times a year, or he may even come to a game once a year but when we see each other, we go to dinner, we talk, it' s just quality time. So I' m real good at being able to get in a conversation with a person and talk to them like

I've been talking to them all year. Then there are my close friends who I talk to a lot.

I've been playing basketball for thirty-one years and it's still fun for me. Maybe not as fun as it was a few years back but it has been such a large part of my life that I know I will miss it when it' s time to move on to something else.

I sure go back and forth on how much longer I'll play. Some times I think two, three years . . . I don't know. I'm getting a little worn down in the sense that I don't like being away from my family. So it would be good if we could permanently live in Texas. I love Texas and my family could be with me while I play.

I wanted to get in the situation . . . For selfish reasons I wanted God to allow me to play long enough so that Avery Jr. could be a ball boy while I'm still playing.

There has been talk for sometime about me being an NBA coach, and I think I have the tools to potentially be a solid coach, but I'm just not sure about the timing. It was nice of Don Nelson to invite me to join the Maverick coaching staff this year after I got hurt, That kind of experience is always a good thing. But I still love to play. At this time I' m a mature basketball player, but I am intrigued with the possibility of coaching full time. One good thing for me is that I have had the good fortune to play for some of the best basketball coaches in the world.

Right now I'm enjoying being part of the Dallas Mavericks. I have spent most of my pro career playing in Texas, and I guess you could call me a Texan by now. The Mavs have some great young players like Dirk Nowitzki, Raef LaFrentz, Nick Van Exel, Steve Nash, and Michael Finley. Dallas is a class organization. Mark Cuban is a great owner who does everything first class and gives you every opportunity to succeed.

Chapter Seventeen

Keep Reaching

Psalm 18:28
"You, O Lord, keep my lamp burning;
my God turns darkness into light."

One thing the event's of September 11th has had on me is to show me that evil is all around us. I think it helps me not to get caught up in my job and other things. There are people because of religious beliefs, and all kinds of things really want to harm other people.

Mario Ellie always said, "stay humble and hungry." There are people struggling out there. So many people were killed! So many kids without fathers! So there are a lot of people hurting because of September 11th, all over.

I see a lot more patriotism now but I think the best thing we can do as a nation, as a world is to go back to the way God commanded us to live, and that's to love one another and to serve Him. We're going to struggle, if the foundation doesn't get stronger.

There's not going to be peace because poverty hurts peace, religious differences hurt peace, racism hurts peace. How can we ever have peace if we have poverty, if we have racism, if there is always fighting between the religions? There are so many people with political agendas that nobody has time to find common ground. When people try to reach out to one another, to love one another like the Bible commands us to do then things will start to change.

God tells us in his Word in II Chronicles 7:14, "If my people, who are called by my name, will humble themselves and pray and seek my face and turn from their wicked ways, then will I hear from heaven and will forgive their sin and will heal their land."

During the fall of 2001 God told me to have a Bible study in my home in Houston for all the NBA players that worked out at the gym with me. And you know of all the dates He told me, September 11th. And that was three weeks before the bombings happened.

That night I had about thirty people at my house and six or seven gave their lives to the Lord. That night I taught on "the secrets to success." Public ally people can make you believe anything but secretly God is watching.

My faith in God really helps me in playing in the NBA because not only do I want to please my coaching staff, my teammates, and my family, but I am also representing the Lord Jesus Christ when I' m out there on the basketball court, and I really want to make Him happy. In the NBA it just feels good to have other believers out there, but I love everybody. Whether you believe in God or not, I love you and that's what God has called me to do.

Pastor Ratliff starts off a lot of his sermons by saying, "God is good." And the congregation says, "All the time." In this world you've always got to hang in there, persevere. A lot of doors are going to close in you face, but new ones will open for you.

No mater who you are, at some point in your life, whether you are a teacher, a preacher, a CEO, a coach, a waitress or waiter, trash man, taxi driver, a nurse or a doctor - someday you will have to reach beyond the break. Don' t stand there holding that broken rope in your hand. REACH! It's a journey not a sprint.

The Beginning

Acclaim For Avery

Proverbs 27:2
"Let another praise you, and not your own mouth; someone else, and not your own lips."

"I identify with a lot of people on this team, especially Avery Johnson. One player in the league made the mistake of saying Avery really didn't belong in the NBA, and could never led a team to a Championship. You know, when I was Governor of Arkansas, that's what they said about me, when I was running for President."

William Jefferson Clinton, President of the United States at a team reception at the White House after the 1999 championship game.

"I first met Avery when we were at Southern University in Baton Rouge. I was a nursing student and a mutual friend, Kevin Florent, who was playing basketball with Avery said he had someone he wanted me to meet. He brought Avery over to my apartment and I liked him from the very beginning. I wasn't much of a basketball fan back then, in fact I didn't even know who Avery Johnson was. I've become a big fan now and really enjoy going to the games.

Little Avery can't get enough of going to the games. He's really into sports. Christanna is a little lady, very feminine. She likes to play with her dolls and dollhouse and likes playing the piano. They keep us both busy.

We have been through a lot together over the years, good times and rough times but we've always stuck together. Avery likes to talk a lot but he's a good listener too. He's a wonderful father and husband. He is a very caring person.

I look forward to building our home in Houston. Whatever Avery wants to do in the future is up to him. If he wants to play some more or go into coaching or what ever that's fine by me."

Cassandra Johnson, Avery's Wife

"Avery was ten years old when I got him. He was from the Lafitte projects. I was at Treme center when a friend of mine came up to me and said, "Hey man, I got some kids that want to play basketball and I'd like you to coach them." He said he had one kid in particular that can play. His name is Avery Johnson.

So I went over and talked to him and asked him if he would come play for me in the NORD. When I first saw Avery walking down the street, he was walking like a gunslinger out of the old west. He walked like a normal kid but he held his hands like a gunslinger. When I first saw him I thought there was something unusual about him. He had a lot of confidence in himself.

I got the team together and Avery was my starting point guard and for his age, he could dribble. He was a very good dribbler.

Everything seemed to come so natural to Avery. He picked things up real fast. He was always a little concerned about his size but I told him, "It wasn't the size of the dog in the fight that mattered. It was the size of the fight in the dog that mattered." He's a real religious person and believes in God. And he practices his faith!

After his time at Southern Avery called me up and told me he was going to be trying out for the NBA. I said, "Man, I'm proud of you. I think you can make it." He said, "You really think I can?" I said, "Yeah, if you set your heart to do something I think you can do it."

I didn't hear from him for a while, but then in September I got a call and he said, "Hoss, I'm going to Southern California to play in a summer league. The Seattle Super Sonics picked me up. I told him to just go out there and do what you can. Leave it on the floor!'

Then it wasn't long after that when he called me up from Dallas. I asked, "What are you doing in Dallas Avery?"

"Well Hoss, you won't believe this . . . I made the team and I'm going to NBA Rookie orientation. He said he wanted to take me to dinner.

When I saw him play his first NBA game I was so proud of him. I didn't say much. You know sometimes when you believe in a person, you think it could happen but you're not really sure. But then when you see it happen you know, this is for real!"

Joe "Hoss" Armant, Avery's Youth Basketball Coach.

"He doesn't back down. He just keeps coming. He has the heart of a champion. AJ always makes his point and we listen. He's a fighter and he keeps us all fighting. He's a very emotional player. He has a huge heart and fights to the end."

Tim Duncan, San Antonio Spurs Forward.

"Avery is . . . I can't say he is a friend because he's more than a friend. I'd like to use the term that he's a brother . . . it's so hard . . . sometimes when I sit down and think, and try to describe our relationship, it's so unique. It's so special, because it is one that is truly unconditional.

At that particular time that you need encouraging, he's there to encourage. When I need some sort of direction, he's there to give me direction. If I need support, he's there to give me support. If at a particular time I need to be told I'm wrong, he tells me I'm wrong. If I need motivation he's there to give me motivation.

He's been an example to me to see how he can live on that level where womanizing and all of the other things that are looked at very casually and seem to be okay to do, for him to be able to keep himself pure and please God in those situations that he's in, I think it is very, very special. The level of temptation that he faces everyday is incredible. It just shows you how much you need Christ in your life to be able to live in that environment. For Avery to be able to do that for all the years he has is very remarkable.

To keep his name good. He stressed that to me from day one about keeping my name good. Those kinds of things are very important to me now. I don't compromise my name for a dollar. I don't compromise my name to get approval from someone. My name is all I have. People are going to love me because it's me.

For me I lean on God and God has placed Avery in my life to lean on him."

Derek Lafayette, Avery's Friend of Friends

"Avery is amazing! I first met Avery when I played pickup ball against him during the summers in Dallas. Avery was good, but you didn't look at him and realize that he was an NBA player. But then I started paying attention to his accomplishments in the league, and it became very obvious, he made up for any possible shortcomings with heart, desire, knowledge of the game, and the ability to communicate on the court and off.

When we acquired Avery in 2002, all those amazing qualities were now part of a veteran who brought every intangible imaginable off the court and a still quick first step that could beat you off the dribble and lay that huge arching left handed layup high off the glass and score when we needed it the most.

Sometimes it seems like there is nothing Avery can't do, and we are proud of what he has contributed to the Mavericks and the city of Dallas."

Mark Cuban, Owner Dallas Mavericks

"I first became aware of Avery when he was the ball boy at Xavier University. He was about ten or eleven years old at the time. He was little but he sure could dribble the ball.

He played at Bell Jr. High and in the recreation leagues and those people were always talking about him. Then he came to St. Aug. He's a giant now compared to what he was when he came to St. Aug.

Avery got his big chance when the state playoffs started. The starting point guard had some difficulties and was suspended so I told Avery, "You're going to start." It wasn't like Avery didn't play that year it was just that we had a great team that we had that year. It was a very talented team. Avery and Donald Royal both ended up in the NBA. We were 35-0 that year.

It wasn't that Avery wasn't a good player. It was just that he was on team with a lot of good basketball players. He's so small and I had only one fear and that was he might get hurt playing with the bigger guys. But when he took a charge he got right back up and kept on going. He could steal the ball and make plays. That team was the only one in Louisiana to ever go undefeated.

If hard work was going to make you successful, Avery was going to be successful. You can see the fruits of his labor now. He would work. In the classroom, outside the classroom, on the basketball floor, he would work.

He was a very good kid and had great parents. He came from the projects now. But it was a different time living in the projects. After those boys graduated I was here for one more year then I moved down to Southern University to coach with my high school coach Bob Hopkins.

Everyone who sees him first says, "Why did you recruit this?" I'd say, "Let em fight and lets see who's standing at the end of the fight. If he ain't the one standing you can get rid of me."

I knew Avery could make it in the NBA if he got a shot at it. I talk to him pretty regularly. We talk about life and different things. I don't get to many of his games because we're playing at the same time he is, but I do see every game I can on TV. He's done a lot for St. Aug. Avery's a giver!

Bernard Griffith, Avery's High School Coach at St. Augustine in New Orleans.

"Avery is the leader of one of the best teams in the NBA."

Jason Kidd, NBA Player

"He's had more owners than an old leather jacket and he's had more coaches than Notre Dame. He's been traded, bought and sold more than a '56 Stud baker."

Dan Cook, Sportswriter Express News

"Avery has been a role model both on and off the court more NBA years than he's willing to admit to me." He is an extroadoriny citizen, and this comes at a time perhaps the exploits and deeds in a more negative sense get the greatest amount of publicity.

David Stern, Commissioner of the NBA

"I love his story. I love his heart. And he's showed everybody he's got the game to be an NBA Champion."

Jim Rome

"Coach Griffith had set up a showcase where he brought in several players from the area for me to take a look at. He really wanted to help Avery get a scholarship. I didn't know any of these kids. I didn't know their names or anything about them. We're always hoping to find a big kid but there was just something about Avery that I liked. I couldn't put a finger on it but there he was of all those players he was the one I liked the most. So I called him over and offered him a scholarship on the spot. You know recruiting is usually a long drawn out process but in this case Avery was grinning from ear to ear. He was ready!

So we went over to his house to meet his parents. I was really impressed with his family. It was pretty obvious they were poor because they were living in the projects but that family was together, his mom and dad and littler sister. They were just good people." I've recruited many kids over the years, and when I met Avery's parents you could just tell he was going to be a good kid—and he was.

The year he was here we had a good team. It wasn't one of our best and it was along way from our worst. He was a wonderful kid to coach, just wonderful. From the first time I met him I could tell he was special and in fact if you believe in the American Dream you know being a good person, working hard and all of that for success well Avery is the poster child for that. As a coach you wish you're whole team could be like him."

Ron Black, Head Coach New Mexico JC

"It's a terrific highlight in a career where you've had to fight. You had to fight all along the way. And that's what life's all about. Congratulations."

David Letterman during an appearance by Avery on The Late Show

"The little motor propelling the San Antonio Spurs through the playoffs (1999) has short, spindly legs, no jump shot, and has been rescued five times from the NBA scrap heap. Why, these very Spurs waived him in 1991 to save $80,000. They re-signed him year later, dumped him again and spent the 1993-94 season bemoaning their lack of a "true" point guard."

Brad Townsend, Staff Writer for The Dallas morning News

"Avery Johnson has demonstrated an extraordinary commitment to the San Antonio Community."

Russ Granik, NBA Deputy Commissioner

"He has just sneaked in and become a very good point guard, a very key player. I think by now people have to realize that you have to guard Avery Johnson, and you do have to treat him with the same kind of respect other point guards get."

Del Harris, Los Angeles Lakers Coach

"Not because he's my brother but he really is a good guy! He was always into sports. Everybody wanted to watch him play because he had such a big heart even though he was always the smallest person playing. We all thought he would be a baseball player. He played both baseball and basketball but at that time he seemed to be more interested in baseball.

I can remember we would always go to the park and watch him play. I was about seven and he was twelve. I was always proud of him. We would cut out from the newspaper clippings anytime his name or his team was mentioned and kept this big scrapbook. He was always very protective of me and till this day he still looks out for me. We kind of protect each other.

When Avery was at Southern we went to every home game. It was very exciting when he turned pro. It wasn't really a surprise to us because we knew he could achieve anything he wanted to achieve. Here it is fourteen years later and he's still going strong. I was so excited when he got married because he met someone who he really loves. It was such an exciting event for us in the family. He has a wonderful wife.

I attend Franklin Avenue Baptist Church. I have had the chance to hear Avery preach and not because he's my brother but he's very good.

Andrea Johnson, Avery's Little Sister

"Guys who don't get drafted or get drafted late have a point to prove. You got all of these lottery picks who make millions, and they don't have to work for it. They just have to sign a big deal. Guys like myself and Avery have to work to get contracts. Every year we have to prove ourselves . . . We take that personal."

Mario Ellie, NBA Player

"Avery represents the true meaning of giving and caring about others"

Ann Wheelock, Chief Operating Officer the Fannie Mae Foundation

"I remember the first time I saw Avery Johnson. He walked into my office and said he was a basketball player. And I think I said something like, "That is very suspect." He was so small. Then I noticed how long his arms were and he had big hands. Then I saw him on the floor and I said, "Yep, he can play all right." That was 1986. It didn't take long to see he could play.

He was very much a pleasant surprise and it just goes to show you . . . I don't think Avery averaged more than seven or eight points a game but he dominated the game. He dominated the conference for two years. He was player of the year two years in a row.

He was a ticket seller. We always sold out at home and when we went on the road it would be a sell out. They came to see him, not the team. We were undefeated for many of those games during that period and when the host team fans realized they were going to loose they started cheering for Avery.

He was always a gracious humble type of kid. Everybody

loved him. He's always been that way. Everyone always loved AJ. If you don't love Avery then you've gotta problem loving.

His great character comes from his parents. He's a charismatic person and I think that's something innate, something you're born with, but his character was developed by his mom and dad. He was sure their off spring. They were class people. Both his mom and dad were class people.

When Avery was here at Southern he was the coach. He was a hard worker. When he was here we ran three offenses. We ran a zone offense, a man to man and then we had the Avery Johnson offense. The players would ask, "Coach, what we going to run tonight? Let's run Avery Johnson." With that offense Avery did what he wanted to do and the other players reacted to him. When we were winning Avery was the coach when we lost I was the coach. Avery has taught me a lot about the game of basketball I tell you that!

When AJ was here we had no discipline problems on the floor or off the floor. I never received any kind of negative report about our basketball players. Never trashing a dorm or tearing up a Coke machine, nothing like that. As soon as AJ graduated all hell broke loose. I couldn't believe what's going on here? Then one day a faculty member told me, "You know that little boy you had here. He had everything under control." He didn't even know Avery's name. He told me of some things he had seen them do and how the little fellow took control.

He's such a great diplomat. Let me tell you how he works. I put in a new offense. Avery always knocked on my door. Most of the players just walk on in. He said, "Coach, can I see you a minute?"

I said, "Sure." He'd say how's your wife? I'd say fine. He'd ask how's your son? He'd go right on down the line then he'd get to it. "Hey coach, you know that new offense you put in the other day? I said, "Yes." He said, "Have you considered . . .?

Now most guys would tell me why they don't like it but AJ was a diplomat, he'd ask, have you considered this or that. What could I say?

When in a ball game, when something goes wrong or we loose he always would take the blame. He would never let his teammates feel that they had let us down.

He was special! He was like the Energizer bunny!

Ben Jobe, Head Coach Southern University

"Before The playoffs in Utah in 1999. "If AJ over Stockton sounds ludicrous—then Utah should telephone Phoenix, The Suns would say they, too, never thought AJ vs Kidd would turn out as it did."

Buck Harvey, writer for the Express News

"I met Avery about 10 years ago through another player, John Turner, when he played for the Houston Rockets. Avery agreed to hire me as his agent representative. At one point he was going to sign a CBA contract because there wasn't an opportunity with an NBA team. I was having lunch with Avery and after I went out to my car and heard on the radio that Tim Hardaway with the Warriors was injured. I called the Warriors right away because I have a strong relationship with Don Nelson. AJ got out there immediately and signed a guaranteed contract, which I believe revitalized his career. It was a beginning to a great future in the NBA. It was a great experience because he had the trust in me to help him in his career.

Avery is the type of person and client that you can't say enough good things about. He's a role model in every sense. He exudes confidence, dedication and love in everything he does in life. He's a wonderful father, athlete, husband, and community activist."

Tony Dutt, Avery's agent

Getting to Know Avery

"Avery, a bunch of people have asked all kinds of questions and I was hoping that you might be willing to take a few minutes and answer some of these. I have to warn you up front that they run the gamut from very trivial to very serious."

"That's fine with me Jimmie. Bring em' on."

"Okay, here we go. A hypothetical one first, if you had not signed with Seattle, and no other team offered you a contract, what kind of profession or business would you have pursued?"

"I was going to be a sales representative for Proctor & Gamble in the states of Mississippi, Arkansas and Louisiana. Coach Jobe had set that up for me, but I'm glad it turned out the way it did."

"Speaking of Coach Jobe the next question does concern him in a way. The question; Coach Jobe is not getting any younger and would you consider taking the coaching job at Southern University if it came open and was offered to you?"

"Well… before they rehired Coach Jobe, some folks from Southern came to see me while I was still playing in San Antonio and offered me the job. I told them it wasn' t the right time for me to get into coaching, that I had a couple of years left, in my NBA career. But I was flattered that they thought enough of me to offer me the job.

When I didn't take the job, they gave me a list of about fifty or so names of people they thought would be good for the job, and asked me to look at the list and recommend someone. I told them I thought Coach Jobe should be rehired. I would always consider the Southern job if it was offered at the right time, but really I see myself as an NBA coach."

"If you were to take a college coaching job how do you think you would handle the recruiting, as many coaches think that that is the hardest part of the job?"

"I don't think that would be a problem for me because I'm a people person. I'm the kind of coach that could walk into a prospects home and really sell the kid and his parents on my program and what I'm all about. I've been that way all of my life. Kids are attracted to me. It's a God given gift. He's given me this gift to find favor with people."

"Do you read the sports page much?"

"During the season I read it six days a week. It doesn't bother me when negative things are written about me, or my team. It use to, but not anymore."

"What is your favorite arena to play in?"

"I like to play in Houston the best. It just seems like I play my best games there. And Cleveland is my least favorite. I just never played well in Cleveland and the incident with Malik always comes back when I go to play there."

"Do you have a shoe contract?"

"Yes, but my first shoe contract was with Avia. My second was with Pony and I had one with Reebok and now I'm with Nike."

"I could answer this one for you Avery. Many of the NBA players are known as fancy dressers. How about you?"

(laughing) "I can be at times. I like to wear suits on the road. When I'm home I like to wear just a shirt and slacks. When

I'm on the road, and the kids are not around, and I have time to get myself organized, that' s when I wear my fanciest cloths. I have my cloths made for me and that helps a lot."

"Do you watch other sports?"

"I love to watch college basketball. But my favorite is watching golf and I like to watch football. I'm a hot and cold Saints fan. I like to watch players, more than teams. I like to watch Chris Carter. I liked to watch Reggie White and John Elway when they were playing. Jerry Rice and Steve Young were some of my favorites but one of my favorite players is my home-boy, Marshall Faluk. I go to the games periodically but mostly I watch them on television."

"Now here's an all- time question. Can you beat Derek at golf?"

"No, not at the present time but when I retire I will!"

"Are any of your children into sports?"

"Yeah, Christiana is playing tennis and she can hit a mean ball and Avery, he's into basketball. I don' t want to sound like a proud father but he is the best six - year old basketball player in the state of Colorado. He can dribble the ball with both hands and he's extraordinarily fast. He' s little, which runs in the family. When I watch him play my heart beats a thousand miles a minute or when I watch my daughter hit a tennis ball."

"What was the first car you ever owned?"

"It was a red Ford Escort. A 1985 Escort that Mr. Norman bought for me."

"Here's a good one, not including the Bible, what is the best book you have ever read?"

"That is tough... probably two books. One is by T.D. Jakes, and it's called, *Loose That Man and Let Him Go.*" And the other is . . . I can't remember the name . . . Pop gave it to me, it' s by Bill Bradley the Senator from New York. The title slips my mind. But it was a very good book."

"What is your favorite television show?"

"I don't watch a lot of television but I do like Law and

Order."

"Do you play video games?"

"Not now, but when I first came in the league with Seattle I was the best video-football game player in town. Now Derek Mckey and Olden Polynice might say different, but that's just them."

"Were you surprised when you started to grow a little in college?"

"I didn't notice it much until my second year in college when I went from 5'3" to 5'6". That was one of my biggest jumps. It felt funny! I was having some problems in terms of my body. I had had a hip injury and was having some knee problems then later looking back I think it was from that growing spurt."

"I knew we'd get this one. Who was your favorite player when you were young?"

"Tiny Nate Archibald. I liked him because he was left - handed and he was short. My second favorite player was "Pistol" Pete Marovich. I got to watch him play when I was a kid growing up in New Orleans. I loved how he handled the ball with his behind the back passes and all. I practiced everyone of his moves."

"Did you ever get to see Dr. J play?"

"I only got to see him play on TV and he was incredible. He was everything I had heard about him before."

"Who do you think was or is the best player ever?"

"Michael Jordan. No doubt, Michael Jordan!"

'Would Bob Cousey be a star in today's NBA?"

"I don't think so...That's a tough question. He'd be a quality player. But with his skill level I don't think he'd be a star, He'd be a starter."

"If they were to make a movie of your life who do you see playing Avery Johnson?"

Smiling, "Probably someone like Cuba Gooding Jr."

"How do you travel to away games?"

"With the Mavericks, we have our own plane. Some of the

other teams have their own planes too or either they fly charter."

"Do wives ever travel with the team?"

"Maybe two or three times a year they get to travel with us. Most teams are pretty good about that. Denver has a policy where they don't allow wives on the airplane."

"I'm sure you stay at the best hotels but are there many autograph seekers hanging around?"

'You're right Jimmie, we stay at the best hotels and there are always autograph seekers hanging around even when we get in at three in the morning. The better your team the more the autograph seekers."

"Do you remember the first time someone asked you for your autograph?"

"I think it was after we lost to Kentucky in the NCAA tournament in my senior year. Some one asked me for my autograph in the hotel lobby in Cincinnati."

"Do you socialize with other teammates families?"

"We go out together after the games, go to dinner. I go out and eat with guys on the road. I was socializing with Adrian Griffin and his wife because I lived in the same building in Dallas. We are people, for some reason or another that attracts people to us. We just seem to be magnets."

"Have you always worn the same number?"

"No, I started out wearing number five with Seattle, then 11 with Denver the first time, then 15 with the Spurs the first time, and the second time. I wore number six with the Rockets and I think I wore number six with Golden State and then I wore six with the Spurs again and six with the Nuggets the second time now I wear five with Dallas. I think I wore 15 in college."

"What did you think the first time you came out of the locker room onto the court for your first NBA game?'

"The first time I came out onto the court in the NBA was in 1988 against the Utah Jazz in the old Salt Palace, not their new arena The Delta Center. When I ran out there, I think I was the first one out there and it was an awesome feeling. I didn't play that night but it still was an awesome feeling. The next night we had back-to-back games with Sacramento. We were beating them when Bernie put me in with a minute or two to go and I scored my first NBA points. That was November 1988 and it was on a right handed shot over Vinny Del Negro who would be my future teammate."

"How about the first time you were introduced as a starter?"

"The first time being introduced as a starter was in my second year at Seattle. Bernie wanted to shake up the lineup a little bit so he started me. I think that game was against the expansion Miami Heat. Now that was exciting! Talk about not being able to sleep. I think I stayed at the arena all night."

"Do you still get that adrenaline rush when you come out and are introduced?"

"Absolutely! Absolutely! It's still exciting. I love it!"

"Do you watch much game film and what are you looking for?"

"I watch a ton of game film. I like to watch game films of other teams. I like to watch previous games that we played in. I look for different things, you know, areas that we are weak offensively and defensively. I look for how we are rotating defensively. Am I keeping my man in front of me? Am I pushing the ball up the court fast enough? Am I calling the right play? I look for certain guys and where they like to operate on the court. Their strengths. Looking to see how they are going to play me with their pick and roll defense. I'm looking for body language to see if a guy really wants the ball or doesn't want the ball."

"How do you call your plays?"

"Well, I think a lot of it is having an idea what the coach wants in terms of ball movement. Then I see who is really cooking, you know, if a guy' s hot on my team. I look at that, and I like to go at match ups. I like to go at bad defenders. That's the philosophy that I like. What are their weaknesses defensively? Sometimes we call the plays by number and sometimes they are just read situations. You know I'm an inside guy. I like to establish the inside."

"Do you call a play every time down the court?"

"Not every time. If I'm calling a play every time that's a problem."

"I hear you are wound pretty tight before a game, is that right?"

"Not as much as I used to be. When my role was a starter with the Spurs I barely said anything to my wife on game day. I was focused. I had to be focused. I had to have an edge. That was my edge. Preparation . . . focus, that was my edge. I didn't want to talk to anybody until after the game. My teammates knew that too."

"Do you have any trouble sleeping the night before a game?"

"I used to. Not so much anymore. I did have some trouble sleeping this year with the Mavericks in the playoffs. Even though I wasn't on the roster I was excited about the playoffs and the coaching opportunity."

"How early before tip off do you arrive at the arena?"

"I like to get to the arena about two hours before game time."

"Do you eat differently on game days?"

"Yeah. In the morning I drink a protein shake. Then I go to the shoot – around and after that I go and have two pancakes or two or three egg whites scrambled well done. Then I take a nap. I eat three and one half hours before game time. So for a 7:30 game I eat at 4 sharp. For a seven o'clock game I eat at 3:30 sharp. I like pasta with grilled chicken. After the game I like to eat fish."

"Who was your favorite sports hero?"

"All sports? Ah...Avery . . .Avery . . . Joh ...my...favorite sports hero...Arthur Ashe...I would probably say Arthur Ash. He was not only a great tennis player he was an outstanding person, so I'd say Arthur Ashe."

"What do you think about the big salaries that athletes are receiving today, are they warranted?"

"Absolutely. But at the same time, I feel teachers should get paid more. And fire-fighters and police even if I had to pay more in my tax dollars. But I think for athletes they are warranted. If the athletes have created a market, and the environment where people are willing to pay that type of money, it' s warranted. They have a special, unique gift and people are paying thousands and thousands of dollars to see them play, yes, I think they are warranted."

" What's your favorite TV show?"

" Probably, Law and Order. But I don't watch much TV."

" How would you like to be remembered?"

Without hesitation. "As a giver. Now you can fix that up any kind of way you want, but that is the way I want to be remembered, as a "giver." With my finances, with wisdom, with instruction, giving a helping hand, an ear, myself. I just want to be remembered as a "giver."

"How is important Christian fellowship to you?'

"It's very important. My mom used to say, 'You are your company.' You can tell a person by the kind of people they hang around with. Christian fellowship is very important because people need help sometimes and maybe I can help them and maybe some of the areas that I'm weak in, they can help me become stronger."

"Do you have a tendency to take anything for granted? The future, a spouse, your salvation?"

"Everybody takes their salvation for granted. You know you're going to heaven, you know you can't lose your salvation so we all take it foe granted."

"Do you think you might go into the Christian ministry full time someday?"

"You know Jimmie, personally, I get asked that question a lot, and I don't want to sound arrogant here or what ever, but I'm in the full-time ministry now. Full time ministry for me is not somebody or a pastor of a church and he' s working fulltime at the church. God has called us all to go into the world and be disciples and visit the prisons, visit the sick. He's called us all to go into the world and preach and witness to share. He' s called us all into this world not to be receivers but to be givers."

"If you could write a proverb of warning to this generation what would it be?"

Probably, to put God first . . . in everything you do. Also, that you reap what you sow. I'm a big believer in that."

"What is your greatest ambition, at this point in your life".

" My greatest ambition . . . to see everybody have a life that is heaven on earth, and when life is over go to heaven."

"What motivates that ambition?"

After seeing poverty, racism, uneducated people, people that are discriminated against, people with low self-esteem and no confidence."

"Any regrets in life?"

"In terms of what, like things I've done?"

"Yes, or maybe, things you haven't done."

"I regret some of the things I've said to people, maybe out of frustration, or whatever the case. I regret some of the things I' ve said to people. But other than that, no regrets."

"Why do you think people reject Gods gift of salvation?"

"Pride, because of pride. It seems too simple to believe. There are so many ideas, so many different religions. People saying there are thousands of ways to get to heaven. People question God."

"When do you feel most loved by God?"

" Probably every time He allows me to wake up in the morning!"

"How do you show your love for God? "

"I would say, mainly, when I resist temptation. Secondly, when I do and say exactly what he wants me to say and do."

"Thanks Avery. That was great and I am sure the readers will be pleased."